Venice
Botteghe

D1519851

Michela Scibilia

Venice
botteghe

antiques, bijouterie, coffee,
cakes, carpets, glass...
a handbook for
self-assured shoppers

www.vianellolibri.com

concept, text, photographs,
maps, graphic design and layout
Michela Scibilia

english translation
Giles Watson

editor
Elisabetta Ballarin
Luisa Bellina
Andrea Montagnani
Chiara Romanelli
Nicolò Scibilia

editorial consultant
Livio Scibilia

fonts and symbols
Scala sans (Martin Majoor, 1993)
Shop (Michela Scibilia
with Elisabetta Ballarin, 2004)

printed by
Grafiche Vianello
Treviso

Special thanks to
Daniele Resini for
allowing the author to
use his superb digital
camera, without which
this guide could not have
been completed.

This guide is dedicated
to all those who continue
to live and work in Venice.

advisors and shopping
companions
Mario Alberti
Chiara Barbieri
Rosa Barovier Mentasti
Annabella Bassani
Cesare Benelli
Ilaria Boccagni
Sandro Borin
Marie Brandolini
Monica Briata
Mauro Bruscagnin
Catherine Buyse Dian
Jonathan Del Mar
Maria Giulia da Sacco
Gaia Donà
Marina Errera
Laura Fregolent
Irina Freguglia
Guido Fuga
Elena Fumagalli
Anna e Giorgio Ferrari
Marina Gattinoni
Luca Grinzato
Cecilia Gualazzini
Giovanni Keller
Alessandra Magistretti
Girolamo Marcello
Vittorio Marchiori
Marta Moretti
Gianfranco Munerotto
Claudio Nobbio
Sili Orsi Bertolini
Monica Pistolato
Marco Saba
Violetta Sandu
Francesca Scarpa
Mariateresa Sega
Adrian Smith
Philippe Trapp
Manuel Vecchina
Andrea Vianello
Sergio Volpe
Jill Weinreich
Neda e Alfredo Zambon

Version 1.1
November 31, 2004

Shopping

An introduction to shopping in Venice could start in any one of
a thousand ways, but there is only one possible final comment:
Venice is a city with commerce in its soul. One thread runs
unbroken from Venice the Mediterranean superpower to Venice
the tourist magnet. Selling things, including the city, is the name
of the game. Everything in Venice risks turning into a souvenir.
There seems to be no escape, but if you look closely, there is still
a part of Venice that refuses to fit into this scheme of things.
It is the Venice that descends directly from the 16th-century
craft schools which made the city not just Europe's centre of
sophistication but also a major hub of manufacturing industry.
Today, we are consumers rather than citizens. A purchase may
count for more than a vote. If that is the case, it will be helpful
to make those purchases in an informed manner. Who knows.
Perhaps the oft-invoked law of supply and demand can take us
back to the quality and refinement of yesteryear.
I have tried to write the kind of guide that I would like to find for
any city I did not know. I want it to be an aid to finding out more
about the goods you see in the shop windows. The guide is a way
of discovering the story behind the merchandise, or perhaps just
what goes into it. It will help you to spot traditional craft products
and appreciate their qualities.
The following pages review many famous shops and workshops,
as well as others that are almost unknown because they have
never attempted to promote themselves. The main criterion for
selection was that there should be someone in the craft workshop
or shop who knows the ins and outs of what is on sale.
Specific, concrete knowledge is a rare commodity in a world
of planning managers and account supervisors.

Otherwise, why shouldn't you use the internet, where endless suppliers are only too willing to deliver your shopping at the click of a mouse? What's the point of buying anything in Venice – with its added inconvenience and transport costs – if you can find it somewhere else? I want to encourage people to seek out the Venice that still exists behind the tourist-trap façade. It is a Venice that doggedly continues to gild picture frames, carve *fòrcola* rowlocks and bake almond-sprinkled *fugassa* loaves while muttering under its breath *"me convegnaria vender mascare de plastega* (I'd be better off selling plastic masks)".

Among all the smoke and mirrors, however, it is still possible to find superb craft workers and expert tradespeople who keep the old traditions alive. Innovation is part of that tradition: new techniques and new products are appearing all the time.

To enter one of these workshops is to step into the unknown. You might find a charmer, a firebrand or a flamboyant eccentric, who can draw you into a new world of wonder. On the other hand, there are the crotchety ones – Venetians call them *rusteghi* – who suspect you want to steal their trade secrets, and scrutinise you like a spaniel guarding a particularly tasty bone.

Venice is a corner of the world like everywhere else, but it is more of a world than other places. "Ethnic" is the adjective that has best fitted Venice for some time, long before it became a way of describing a type of cuisine or a fashion in clothing. All the objects that Venetian traders and freebooters have brought back to the city over the centuries are returned to the 14 million tourists from all over the globe who visit each year. Everything is in Venice and Venice is everywhere.

The *calli* and *campielli* contain all that is traditional in Venetian crafts – gondolas, glass, beads, cakes, sweets and fabrics – as well as tempting exotic items such as Persian carpets, mosque lamps, colourful chinoiserie and porcelain, not to mention the most recent additions, like masks, paper, accessories and photographs.

By its very nature, Venice is an international city with an enviable
capacity to welcome visitors. It is hardly fragile. Venice naturally
absorbs everything that is odd, eccentric or merely characteristic,
even if it comes from abroad.
This means Venice has the potential to be the ideal city for craft workers,
artists and professionals. Venice's past could make it the city of the future.
In Venice, there is still a direct, daily contact with other people.
Venetians meet friends and strangers and perhaps take a stroll,
or go for a *spritz* together, chatting about people, boats and work,
as used to be the case in every village. Yet at the same time, Venice
has a concentration and depth of activities that is hard to imagine.
The university, the libraries, the archives, the museums, the Biennale
in its various flavours – visual arts, architecture, film, dance, music
and theatre – and a thousand other events throughout the year all
attract an inquisitive audience of people who appreciate the advantages
and difficulties of this astounding city.

The important thing is not to yield to modernisation. The real Venice needs
to be promoted, without the superfluous addition of elements for which
the city is unsuited. We have to understand that Venice can be modern and
prosperous without having modernity or prosperity forced upon it from
outside. This is the only way forward, if we are to avoid the much-feared
"Veniceland" option of a city that begins and ends with tourism.
Eating convenience foods, buying plastic gondolas made in Taiwan,
or hiring a motorboat to go a few hundred metres along a canal is not
only unmodern, it is positively silly.
Once the most fragile part of the city has been destroyed, it cannot
be put back together, as sociologists and town planners well know.
Venice is made up of the men and women that bring it to life because
they have chosen this very special place to live and embraced its lifestyle.
Will we all end up renting rooms in period costume, or at the helm
of a waterbus full of tourists? I wouldn't rule it out.
But not without a fight!

ANOTHER *BÒVOLETO*

botteghe

● coffee

In the late 16th century, Venice was the first city in Europe to "discover" coffee, which it imported straight from Arabia. At first, it was used as a medicine to *star svegli* (stay awake) before becoming a cult beverage, enjoyed in agreeable surroundings and company. Until a few decades ago, there were many Venetian coffee roasters, some of them tiny, who imported their own beans. Customers would sip their coffee seated among piles of pungently perfumed sacks. Today, only a few purveyors of the *nigra bevanda*, or "dark drink", are left.

Caffè del Doge ▶ G

San Polo 609, calle dei Cinque, +39 +39 041 5227787, closed Sunday (7–19)

Although it opened only recently, the Caffè del Doge is already a very firm favourite with gourmets and, indeed, everyone else. Even the old ladies in the neighbourhood are now coffee experts. If you want an espresso, you can choose from the *Doge Rosso* and *Doge Nero* blends, or nine unblended varieties, including Mexican Altura, Cuban Caracolillo, Ethiopian Sidamo and the sublime Jamaican Blue Mountain. Nor should you neglect Huehuetenango, a Slow Food presidium variety from Guatemala. Also on offer are fresh fruit juices (apple with banana, celery or carrot), extra thick or regular hot chocolate, cakes, pastries, including feather-light meringues with cream, and savoury appetisers.

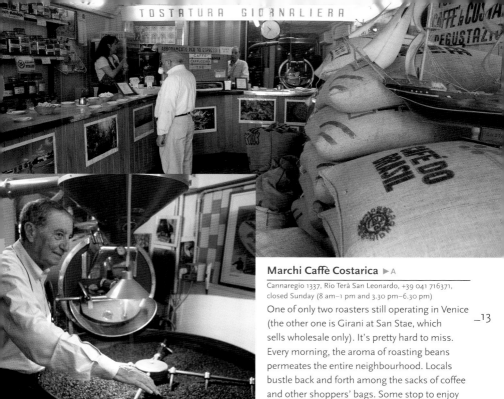

Marchi Caffè Costarica ▸ A

Cannaregio 1337, Rio Terà San Leonardo, +39 041 716371, closed Sunday (8 am–1 pm and 3.30 pm–6.30 pm)

One of only two roasters still operating in Venice (the other one is Girani at San Stae, which sells wholesale only). It's pretty hard to miss. Every morning, the aroma of roasting beans permeates the entire neighbourhood. Locals bustle back and forth among the sacks of coffee and other shoppers' bags. Some stop to enjoy a *caffè della sposa*, "bride's coffee", obtained from a blend of eight of the finest Arabian beans. Others might enquire about a couple of hectograms of Costa Rica to go. A smiling Camillo looks on from the back of the shop.

_13

India ▸ M

Dorsoduro 2964, Campo Santa Margherita, + 39 041 5228924, closed Wednesday afternoon and Sunday (9 am–1 pm and 4.30 pm–7 pm)

A lovely shop that complements coffees from the India roaster at Martellago with a vast selection of teas both packed and loose, including black, green, aromatised and even the stunningly expensive (€ 30 per 100 g) white tea. It's prepared from the tips of shoots picked over a two-day period only twice a year. According to those in the know, white tea should be served with savoury dishes or dried fruit and nuts. It seems that it reinforces the immune system, stimulates the metabolism of carbohydrates, imbues the brain with energy, prevents tooth decay, protects against viruses and bacteria, encourages coagulation of the blood and heals the skin, as well as keeping body tissues supple. Well, if they say so.

WHITE TEA

 # dolci

"As day breaks, I shout hot *zaletto*, boiling hot, hot with raisins'". This was how in the 18th century Gaetano Zompini described, in his *Le Arti che Vanno per Via nella Città di Venezia* (The Street Traders' Guilds of Venice), the *scaletèr,* or pastry cook, so called from the ancient custom of cutting a ladder (*scala*) pattern on sweet bakery products. He sells *zaléti* biscuits to *mogiar nel vin dolse* (dunk in sweet wine), or in a *cicara* of hot chocolate, the traditional destiny of *baìcoli* and *bussolài*. These are all biscuits you can still find in pastry shops and many bakeries, along with *pan dei dogi*, almond and candied fruit-stuffed *moro* or *pevarini* flavoured with honey, cloves, ginger, cinnamon, nutmeg and black pepper. In spring, you will find *fugassa venexiana*, a leavened, almond-sprinkled loaf fragrant with iris root, orange peel, cinnamon, vanilla and cloves. The traditional cake in the *sestiere* (district) of Castello, which had a large community from Greece and the Balkans, is the *greca*, a light, square-shaped almond confection. At Carnival, there are *frìtole* and *galàni* in all the shops. It seems that the guild of *fritoleri*, who sold doughnut-like fritters in the streets of 18th-century Venice, had to pay kickbacks in kind to the evidently sweet-toothed magistrates, the *Provveditori di Comun*, in order to "obtain permission to fry in the *campi* (squares)".

14—

BUSSOLÀI
BURANÈI

ESSI

FRÌTOLE

GALÀNI

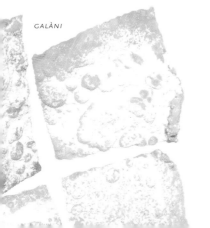

CASTAGNOLE

PINZA

SAN MARTINO

baìcoli thin, light, moderately sweet biscuits that go extremely well with *zabaiòn*

bussolài buranèi (from Burano) ring-shaped biscuits made with egg (the S-shaped variations are known as *essi buranèi*) for dunking into wine

bussolài ciosòti the less sweet Chioggia version of *bussolài buranèi*

castagnole sweets for Carnival

colombina a sweet Easter focaccia

cràf the Venetian version of doughnuts, called *krapfen* in Italian

crèma frìta a custard of eggs, milk, flour and sugar, covered in breadcrumbs and then fried

curasàn the idiosyncratic Venetian pronunciation of croissant

fave dei morti or **favette dolci** "the beans of the dead" are prepared in Italy for the feast of All Souls on 2 November. The Venetian version is made with pine nuts instead of almonds

frìtole fritters with raisins and pine nuts, traditionally made for Carnival

fugàssa (Italian *focaccia*) flat bread

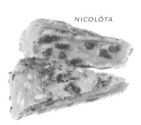

NICOLÒTA

galàni thin sheets of fried sweet pastry, traditionally made for Carnival. In other regions of Italy, they are known as *crostoli*

golosèsso a delicacy

nicolòta a traditional sweet made from stale bread, milk, flour, raisins and fennel seeds

pan dei dogi an oblong biscuit made from dough kneaded with wine, almonds, raisins and pine nuts, then decorated with almonds

persegàda quince preserve known in Italian as *cotognata*. It is made in the shape of a man on horseback for the feast of Saint Martin on 11 November

pìnza a cake with very ancient origins, made today with corn flour. For the feast of the Epiphany on 6 January, it is decorated with fennel seeds, raisins, dried figs and candied peel

CRÈMA TO MAKE CRÈMA FRITA

San Martino The feast of St Martin on 11 November is celebrated with this large, shortcrust biscuit baked in the shape of a man on horseback and decorated with coloured sweets. Children beating pots and pans do the rounds of the neighbourhood singing traditional songs and demanding sweets

spumìlie meringues

tiramisù or **tirimesù** is a sweet invented in the 1950s in the Treviso area. It is made with layers of coffee-soaked biscuits and custard with mascarpone cheese, sprinkled with unsweetened powdered cocoa. The name means "pick-me-up", which is precisely what the combination of coffee and calories is designed to do.

zabaiòn a custard of egg yolk, sugar and sweet fortified wine, the Italian *zabaglione* or *zabaione*

zaléti typical yellow-coloured biscuits made with corn flour, sugar, eggs and raisins

_15

ZALÉTI

CURASÀN

Bonifacio ▶I

Castello 4237, Calle degli Albanesi, + 39 041 5227507, closed Thursday (7.30 am–8.30 pm)

As you are waiting to order a tray of cakes, let yourself be tempted by Bonifacio's generously topped mini pizzas, perhaps with a bracing glass of *spritz* or an Americano cocktail. Be sure not to forget your cakes as you leave, suitably cheered and refreshed.

CRÀF

BAVARIAN CREAM

Boscolo ▶A

Cannaregio 1818, Rio Terà San Leonardo, +39 041 720731, closed Monday (6.30 am–8.30 pm)

Fragrant *curasàn* and warm apple or ricotta-filled turnovers are on hand for a hearty breakfast, as well as mini pizzas and vegetable quiches for those with a space to fill before lunch. The wide range of specialties includes a ring-shaped chocolate Bavarian cream.

MINI PASTRIES

Didovich ▶H

Castello 5908, Campo Santa Marina, +39 041 5230017, closed Sunday (6.30 am–8 pm)

The strawberry Bavarian cream or the chocolate puff? That is the question. There's always a huge selection of cakes, petits fours, millefeuille pastries, Sacher cakes and fruit *semifreddo* desserts to take home with you. The chocolate or zabaglione-filled puffs are irresistible, as are the tempting custard cornets. In summer, these triumphs of the kitchen can be enjoyed while sitting at one of the tables in the *campo* (square).

STRAWBERRY AND
CUSTARD CUP

PUMPKIN CUP

Gobbetti ▶M

Dorsoduro 3108/b, Ponte dei Pugni, +39 041 5289014, open all week (7.15 am–1 pm and 3 pm–8 pm)

Food lovers know it well. Cognoscenti appreciate the lemon, prosecco or zabaglione cakes, the pear cake (guaranteed nothing like your aunt's version), *tiramisù* and unusual bite-sized tarts with pumpkin, pears or custard, not to mention the surprisingly delicate Swiss roll-type sweets. But the signature confection is called Bomba, for obvious reasons, as weightwatchers will regretfully note. It's a hemispherical chocolate-covered chocolate mousse, no less!

LEMON CUP

BOMBA

CHOCOLATE-COVERED
CANDIED ORANGE PEEL

Marchini ►H

San Marco 676, Spadaria, + 39 041 5229109,
closed Tuesday (9 am–8 pm)

The celebrated cake shop at Santo
Stefano closed some time ago.
This one is a favourite with Japanese
visitors taking a break from designer-label
shopping in the neighbourhood.
The petite packages of chocolates come in all colours
and shapes, such as masks or pyramids.
You'll also find *zaléti, baicoli*, Venetian focaccia, *fave,
pan dei dogi* and chocolate covered candied peel.
The meringue and Sacher cake, also available in small
formats, are made by the owners.

SACHER

Martini ►A

Cannaregio 1302, Rio Terà San Leonardo, +39 041 717375,
closed Friday (6 am–9 pm)

A firm favourite with locals for its courteous service,
fragrant honey, blueberry, wholemeal or almond horns,
and tempting mini pizzas, on sale from 10 am.

_17

Melita ►R

Castello 1000, Fondamenta Sant'Anna, no telephone, closed Monday (8 am–2 pm and 3.30 pm–8 pm)

An unashamedly authentic neighbourhood cake shop
in working-class Venice. People come from as far away
as San Marco or even Santa Croce to
buy meringues, *tiramisù* and
fugassa at holiday time.

MERINGUE

TIRAMISÙ

Dal Nono Colussi ►M

Dorsoduro 2867a, Calle Lunga San Barnaba, +39 041 5231871,
closed from Monday to Wednesday (9 am–1 pm and 4 pm–7.30 pm);
often closed on other days as well, and from June to September.
He's more likely to be working during the holidays. Artists are like that!

"Grandfather Colussi" claims to be the oldest pastry cook
in town. There's no denying that he has been baking for six
decades, which is why he takes things easy these days. If you
are in Campo San Barnaba, and your nose happens to start
twitching at the aroma of a focaccia that takes you back to
your infancy, follow the fragrance and you will find Grandfather
Colussi busy at his oven. The focaccias, the apple and black
cherry cake, the tarts and the chocolates are all to die for.

JAM TART

RICE CUP

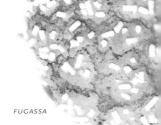

FUGASSA

FLAKY PASTRY FAN

Puppa ▶C

Cannaregio 4800, Salizada del Spezier, +39 041 5237947,
closed Monday (7 am–1 pm and 3 pm–8.30 pm)

This small shop is much appreciated for its traditional bakery products and one or two specialties, such as the *crostella*, a melt-in-the-mouth flaky pastry with whipped cream and chunks of chocolate. First thing in the morning, there are buttery *curasàn* and rice baskets. Later on, flaky pastry or bread-based pizzas appear. Savoury *panettone* is also available to order. This is a kind of large loaf made up of 30 or so small sandwiches with various fillings. Just the thing for a party, or to go with aperitifs before dinner.

FAVETTE

APPLE TURNOVER

Rizzardini ▶G

San Polo 1415, Campiello dei Meloni, + 39 041 5223835, closed Tuesday (7 am–8.30 pm)

One of the last shops not to have been subjected to the attentions of interior decorators. The service can be a little off-hand, but enjoy the superb hot chocolate and the fine range of small cakes and biscuits – the *lingue di suocera* (mother-in-law's tongues) are extra special – almond cake and greca.

CHOCOLATE ROLL

Rosasalva ▶H

San Marco 951, Calle Fiubera, +39 041 5210544, closed Sunday (8 am–8 pm)

Rosasalva is undoubtedly the city's largest maker of cakes, pastries and sandwiches. The *curasàn* are good, and don't miss the little semolina puddings. The shop does the catering for many of Venice's events, so at lunchtime you can find tempting pasta or rice dishes, made in the large kitchens next door, to eat at the counter.

SPUMÌLIE

Targa ▶G

San Polo 1050, Ruga del Ravano, +39 041 5236048, closed Monday (6 am–8 pm)

A stone's throw from the Rialto market is Targa, a great place for a restorative cappuccino if you are doing the shopping. As well as fine *curasàn*, it offers giant *spumìlie*, *pan dei dogi* and an excellent *fornarina*, a glazed flower-shaped focaccia with marzipan, almonds and sugar

HAZELNUT
CREAM CUP

Toletta ▶N

Dorsoduro 1192, Calle della Toletta, +39 041 5227451, open all week (7 am–7.45 pm)

The busy *calle* (street) that leads to the Accademia is where you will find this tiny pastry shop, much-admired for its bite-sized cakes and excellent fruit *semifreddo* desserts.

18_

The delectable **caramèi col stecco** are wooden skewers with pieces of toffee-covered fresh or dried fruit. They used to be sold in the streets by vendors from Cadore. Nowadays, you can find them at
La Maison de la Crêpe ▶ H

Cannaregio 5781, Salizada San Giovanni Grisostomo, +39 041 2770565, open all week (10 am–11 pm)

CARAMÈI

Tonolo ▶ F

Dorsoduro 3764, Calle San Pantalon, +39 041 5237209,
closed Sunday afternoon and Monday (7.45 am–8.30 pm)

A firm favourite with many for the quality and variety of its sweet and savoury confections, not to mention its attractive prices. The cake counter goes on forever. Coffee puffs are followed by mini puffs, cakes, millefeuille and *mimosa* cake – with chocolate cream, sponge and cream – or a classic meringue, *greca*, Sacher or *fugassa*. During Carnival, queues form as the sweet-toothed line up for fritters and *galani*.

Trevisan ▶ F

_19

Santa Croce 636, Calle Sechera, +39 041 720713, closed Saturday afternoon and Sunday (7 am–8 pm)

A bakery and cake shop with tables outside. The *curasàn* are good. Don't miss the *pane di Merano*, black bread made with rye and fennel seeds. Younger customers might enjoy a *Casper*, a milk roll in the shape of the cartoon ghost.

CORNET

Vio ▶ F

Santa Croce 784, Fondamenta Rio Marin, +39 041 718523, closed Wednesday (6.30 am–8.30 pm)

The baton has passed from Gilda to her daughter Sonia, who effortlessly keeps the family flag flying. The unusual cakes sold by the metre are a marvellous idea. Choose from chestnut or jam tart, *tiramisù* or the extra-special fresh fruit tart and rum meringue. Vio's savoury baking is also very tempting, particularly the Parmesan cheese shortcrust biscuits.

PUFF

 ice cream

Venetians and Arabs both claim to have invented the sorbet, the forerunner of the ice cream. But the gelato that people used to enjoy in Venice followed the tradition of the ice cream makers from the Zoldo valley and Cadore.

Today, the law permits greater product variety, provided the shop stays within a single category of merchandise, in this case foodstuffs. Many milk bars and fritter friers have discovered a vocation to be "craft-made ice cream shops", or sell pizzas by the piece to undiscriminating tourists.

El Todaro ▶P

Piazza San Marco 3, +39 041 5285165, closed Monday winter only (8 am–8 pm)

The oldest ice cream shop in town. For almost 60 years, El Todaro has been serving ice creams to go and heart-stoppingly expensive sundaes at its tables. Amuse yourself by watching the tour guides desperately trying to keep their groups together.

Da Nico ▶N

Dorsoduro 922, Zattere, +39 041 5225293, closed Thursday (6.45 am–10 pm)

With the first timid rays of spring sunshine, Venetians crowd the Zattere to savour one of Nico's ice creams, either on the hoof or at one of the tables. Most in demand are the *gianduiotto*, a slice of hazelnut ice cream in a glass of whipped cream, or *panna in ghiaccio*, an iced cream sandwich.

Alaska ▶F

Santa Croce 1159, Calle Larga dei Bari, +39 041 715211, closed Monday winter only (12 am–12 pm)

Carlo Pistacchi (yes, the name does mean "Charlie Pistachio") is a born experimenter and a stickler for quality. His small ice cream shop has space for all the classics, from *fior di latte* (top of the milk) and hazelnut to – real – chocolate, according to season and inspiration. Strawberry, pear, fig, fennel, artichoke, celery, asparagus, ginger, green tea, azuki bean, wasabi, cinnamon, malt and cardamom ice creams are all made with fresh whisked or centrifuged raw materials. In summer, try the crushed ice *granita* made with lemon or orange juice.

Lo Squero ►N

Dorsoduro 990, Fondamenta Nani, +39 041 2413601, open all week (10.30 am–9 pm)

When the sun is in the sky, and it would be a shame to stay indoors, ice cream lovers saunter into Simone's shop and pick up a cone to enjoy on the benches at the Zattere. Don't miss the Sicilian pistachio, the Piedmont hazelnut or the exotic Australian Maccadamia. In wintertime, Simone can't keep up with demand for his plain chocolates with chilli pepper, figs or dates.

Millevoglie ►F

San Polo 3033, Frari, +39 041 5244667, open all week (10 am–12 pm)

If you are in the Frari area, you'll observe that most people are eating an ice cream. All the creamy versions are good, especially the luscious Venetian cream, *tiramisù* and *bacio* flavours.

Fantasy ►H

San Marco 929, Calle dei Fabbri, +39 041 5225993, open all week (10 am–8 pm, until midnight in summer)

Only recently opened, but already much frequented by local office and shop workers. The classic flavours sell well, but aficionados recommend the diet-busting *crema del doge*, with chocolate-veined confectioner's cream, and the zabaglione.

La Boutique del Gelato ►H

Castello 5727, Salizada San Lio, +39 041 5223283, open all week (10 am–12 pm)

Small but extremely popular. Cream flavours are most requested, especially hazelnut.

Il Gelatone ►B

Cannaregio 2063, Rio Terà della Maddalena, +39 041 720631, open all week (10.30 am–11 pm)

A mandatory stop for many of the commuters heading for the station each afternoon. Interesting offerings include yoghurt, sesame and honey ice cream, not to mention the refreshing aniseed and mint, or pink grapefruit, sorbets.

Il Pinguino ►Q

Castello 2141, Riva San Biagio, +39 041 2411395, open all week (11 am–11 pm)

After a brisk stroll from San Marco to the Arsenale, you certainly deserve an ice cream. The specialty here is called *Mamma Mia*, vanilla and peach ice cream with almond macaroons. You can sit down on the Riva to enjoy both it and the stupendous view, moored yachts permitting.

bread

BOVOLO

Just beyond Riva degli Schiavoni, in Riva Ca' di Dio, there is an eccentric-looking building with late Gothic crenellations. It is one of the many *forni da biscotto* (biscuit bakers) that once stood in the Arsenale area, many others having been knocked down to make way for the Palasport. They were state-run ovens where the bakers, often German, would bake the rusks, or *pan biscotto*, for the ships' crews to give them something *to tociàr* (dunk) in their milk or soup on board. The traditional everyday bread made with white flour was the *bòvolo*, a loaf in the shape of a snail (*bòvolo* in Venetian), as can be seen in the ancient

22–

mosaics in San Marco. Similar to Italian rosebud-shape *rosette*, *bòvoli* can be spotted on the tables of the various versions of the *Last Supper* painted in Venice, from Veronese to Tintoretto. Among the other kinds of bread were *bine*, two small loaves joined like Siamese twins, buttock-shaped *ciope* (or *ciape*) and *filoni* made up of three loaves joined together. The more modern, well-leavened *rosetta*, popular until a short time ago, is shaped like a flower with a central bud and petals opening around it. Equally traditional breads were the *montasù* and the *dressa*, a soft milk loaf glazed with beaten egg. Nowadays, Venice's bakeries, like those in the rest of Italy, use fast-acting yeasts and flours that tend to be over-refined.

ROSETTA

CIOPA

STANGHETA

MONTASÙ

MATO

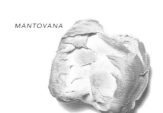

MANTOVANA

BREADSTICKS

CIABATTA

However, quality and variety are good. Every bakery makes dozens of different kinds of bread every day, from the fragrant *ciabatta* to the soft, sweet *ambrogino*. The plain, least expensive bread – when there is any – runs out early in the morning. Still, you will always find loaves with raisins, olives, rice flour, potato flour, bran or sesame seed. These are certainly tasty, but can cost twice as much as ordinary bread. Naturally leavened bread arrives every day from the mainland, and you will find it on sale at organic food shops.

WHOLEMEAL LOAF

POTATO BREAD

MILK BREAD

BREAD WITH OLIVES

Volpe ▶ A

Cannaregio 1143, Ghetto Vecchio, +39 041 715178, closed Sunday (6 am–1 pm and 5 pm–7.30 pm)

We mention this bakery because in addition to the types of bread listed above, it also sells kosher bread certified by the rabbi of Venice. The breads on sale include unleavened bread and Jewish bakery products without salt, yeast or animal fats, *orecchiette di Aman* (pasta triangles filled with plum and poppy seeds, then fired) unleavened cakes with fennel, snake-shaped *bisse*, *impade* (filled with almond paste), macaroons, sugar cakes and, at Jewish New Year, the bread-like *Bollo*.

AMARETTO

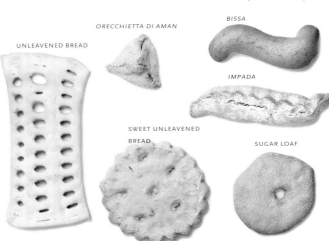

UNLEAVENED BREAD

ORECCHIETTA DI AMAN

BISSA

IMPADA

SWEET UNLEAVENED BREAD

SUGAR LOAF

pasta

The Venice of craft workers was so varied that it gave rise to an incredible range of terminology, which is reflected in the city's place names and a specific vocabulary.

The *forneri* and *pistòri* were the bread makers, *scaletèri*, *buzoladi* and *fritolèri* were pastry cooks and doughnut makers while the *lasagnèri* made pasta. Venetians have always been great consumers of rice, but were not averse to pasta, both dry and fresh (in *Una Delle Ultime Sere di Carnovale*, 18th-century playwright Carlo Goldoni's characters eat *rafiòi*, *ravioli* filled with herbs and *ricotta*).

Pasta *fina*, *menueli* and *lasagnète* went into soups. *Tagiadele*, *lasagne* and *ziti* were for oven-baked *pastizzi*. *Bìgoli*, thick, rough-textured spaghetti made with soft, generally wholemeal flour, were garnished with *salsa*, the slow-cooked anchovy and onion sauce that was served on days of abstinence from meat.

TAGLIOLINI AROMATISED WITH CUTTLEFISH INK, SPINACH, TOMATO, BEETROOT, CHILLI PEPPER AND GARLIC, PLAIN (EGG) AND CURRY

POTATO GNOCCHI

GNOCCHETTI TRICOLORI

RAVIOLI

TORTELLINI

TORTELLONI

PLAIN AND CHILLI PEPPER AND GARLIC SPAGHETTI ALLA CHITARRA

Rizzo ▶ H

Cannaregio 5778, Salizada San Giovanni Grisostomo, +39 041 5222824,
closed Sunday and Wednesday afternoon (8.30 am–1 pm and 3 pm–7.30 pm)

Renowned for its fresh pasta, Rizzo was the first to sell the
aromatised, coloured pastas that today grace many of Venice's
food shop windows. The now classic black tagliolini, with
cuttlefish ink, or the pink, salmon-flavoured version, have been
joined by more exotic shapes and colours, such as Curaçao blue
and blueberry. Rizzo also offers a wide range of packaged fine
food products from all over the world, including Chinese and
Indian rice, Japanese spices, Mexican sauces and more besides.

Le Spighe ▶ Q

Castello 1341, Via Garibaldi, +39 041 5238173, closed Sunday (10.30 am–1 pm and 5.30 pm–7.30 pm)

Doriana is not one to compromise. She makes excellent fresh pasta,
using only fresh natural ingredients in season for her tagliolini, *bigoli*,
ravioli and tortellini. Venice's most prestigious hotels vie for her pasta.
The shop also offers a good selection of fresh organic foodstuffs.

La Dispensa ▶ G

_25

San Polo 376, Ruga del Spezier, +39 041 5231700, closed Wednesday afternoon
and Sunday (9 am–1 pm and 4.30 pm–7 pm)

Pastas from Le Spighe (see above) and lots of nice things from
small-scale organic producers. Busy, especially during market hours.

Serenissima ▶ I

Castello 3455, Salizada dei Greci, +39 041 5227434, closed Sunday (8 am–1 pm and 5 pm–7.30 pm)

Ivan De Rossi makes mainly fresh pasta, tagliatelle, lasagne, potato and semolina gnocchi,
tortellini, agnolotti and ravioli, but he also turns his hand to oven-baked *pasticcio alla bolognese*
or *pasticcio con radicchio e gorgonzola*.
On Thursdays, you'll find his ricotta and spinach-filled potato roll and on Fridays pasta envelopes
filled with basil and hazelnuts, pumpkin, radicchio, artichoke or asparagus, according to the season.
When the warm weather arrives, he whips up a rice salad or two.

ANGEL HAIR PASTA

TAGLIOLINI

TAGLIATELLE

PAPPARDELLE

organic, ethical and the like

As in other cities, increasing attention is focused in Venice on organic products. Organic shops offer goods that are not made by large multinationals, the firms that make the rich even wealthier and bleed the rest of us dry. They also provide good advice and suggestions for healthy, balanced eating. It is worth noting the quality and authenticity policy promoted by Coop supermarkets. Members of the group have a system of transparency and quality control. Increasingly, Coop outlets are selling ethical products from small co-operative enterprises in the world's south.

Baldrocco ▶ B

Cannaregio 2000, Rio Terà de la Maddalena, +39 041 718685,
closed Sunday (9 am–1 pm and 5 pm–8 pm)

This fruiterer always has plenty of organic fruit and vegetables. There is also a selection of packaged food and some detergents. Another plus is the nearby *riva* landing, handy for water-borne transport.

Il Punto Biologico ▶ I

Castello 6651, Barbaria de le Tole, +39 041 5228037,
closed Sunday (9 am–2 pm and 5 pm–8 pm)

Part of this large store is still a *biavaròl*, a traditional neighbourhood food shop that sells almost anything you could want. The ever-courteous Fulvia is on hand to suggest organic and biodynamic products, fruit, vegetables and cheeses, as well as packaged foods.

Rialto Biocenter ▶ G

San Polo 366, Campo de le Becarie, +39 041 5239515, closed Wednesday afternoon and Sunday (8.30 am–1 pm and 4.30 pm–8 pm)

The only organic store that has just about everything, from baby products to a good range of packaged and frozen foods, in addition to cosmetics and some cleaning products.
On Mondays, Wednesdays and Fridays, there are deliveries of farm-fresh fruit, vegetables, eggs, milk and cheese.
Every day, you'll find a fine selection of breads made with spelt, oats, millet, wholemeal flour, cereals and more besides.

Rio Bio ▶ F

Santa Croce 1628, Campo San Giacomo dall'Orio, +39 041 718913,
closed Sunday (9 am–1 pm and 4.30 pm–7.30 pm)

Beauty products, essential oils, food supplements, soap powder, pasta, rice, cereals, biscuits and small selection of fresh organic products like milk, cheese and tofu.

Cibele ▶ B

Cannaregio 1823, Campiello dell'Anconeta, +39 041 5242113,
closed Sunday (8.30 am–12.45 pm and 3.30 pm–7.45 pm)

Natural foods for grown-ups and children, medicinal herbs and
extracts, Bach flowers and herbal beauty treatments. There's
a good selection of herbal infusions, pasta, cereals and biscuits,
as well as fresh bread, tofu, cheese, milk including rice milk,
and soy shoots. But above all, you'll appreciate the helpfulness
and wide knowledge of foods, natural cures and macrobiotics.

Rio Terà dei Pensieri ▶ S

Giudecca 712, Fondamenta de le Convertite, info +39 041 2960658, open every Thursday morning

This co-operative society provides training for the inmates of Venice's jails. Every Thursday morning
on the Giudecca's Fondamenta delle Convertite, they set up a vegetable stall where you can purchase
organic products from a superb garden, which extends over more than 6,000 square metres, inside
the women's jail. On offer are fruit and vegetables in season, as well as fine-quality aromatic
and medicinal herbs that inmates use to make a range of cosmetics.

La Terra di Baba Yaga ▶ Q

Castello 1727, Via Garibaldi, +39 041 2960801, closed Sunday (10 am–1.30 pm and 3 pm–8.30 pm)

Brunella is the woman locals come to when they want organic or biodynamic
products. She has packaged foods, products for the home and wonderful
vegetable-dyed things to wear made from natural fibres, not to mention
hemp slippers.

Bottega della Solidarietà ▶ H

San Marco 5164, Campo San Bartolomeo, +39
041 5227545, open all week (9.30 am–8 pm)

The "Solidarity Shop" is the outlet for
the fair trade network that distributes
products from developing countries.
You'll find teas, herbal infusions,
chocolate, spices, sauces, coffee,
preserves, clothing accessories,
household ornaments and intriguing
ethnic toys made from recycled
tin cans.

essences, herbs and spices

Before there were any of the modern methods of conserving food, spices were both ferociously expensive and vital for survival. In the 14th century, there were 15 spice merchants in Venice. Rialto hosted a wholesale market where every day the *messeri del pepe* fixed the price of the spices unloaded from cargo ships arriving from the east. Their representative then got onto on a pedestal over the statue of the Gobbo, or hunchback, in front of the church of San Giacometto, to read out the prices that would be applied. Those days have gone, but you can still find good curry, ginger, turmeric, various kinds of cinnamon, paprika and much else besides.

Spezieria all'Ercole d'Oro ▶ B

Farmacia Santa Fosca, Cannaregio 2233, Salizada Santa Fosca, +39 041 720600, closed Saturday afternoon and Sunday (9 am–12.30 pm and 3.45 pm–7.30 pm)

Who knows whether you can still get the "Pills of the Priest of Santa Fosca" that in 1701 made the fortune of naturalist, pharmacist, chemist and botanist Giovanni Girolamo Zannichelli.
You will find henna, mallow, blueberry, mustard, pollen, mate and yarrow, and will have a chance to admire the superb, lovingly conserved pharmacy with its original 17th-century furnishings and Sansovina-style beams.

Il Melograno ▶ M

Dorsoduro 2999, Campo Santa Margherita, +39 041 5285117, closed Sunday (9.30 am–1 pm and 4 pm–7.45 pm)

Campo Santa Margherita is a big, noisy square, swarming with three-wheelers, kids, skateboards, footballs and yelling mothers. Thankfully, Maria Rosaria Limongelli is in her shop with quiet advice on herbal beauty treatments and other products.
Mind you, she's quite likely to recommend an inexpensive remedy, or even one that doesn't cost anything at all!

PINE NUTS

SULTANAS

Màscari ▶ G

San Polo 381, Ruga del Spezier, +39 041 5229762, closed Sunday and Wednesday afternoon (8 am–1 pm and 4 pm–7.30 pm)

An address to note for anyone who wants to try traditional, sophisticated or exotic recipes. There are gelatines, almonds, walnuts, pine nuts, wheat, sunflower seeds, candied fruit, sultanas, dried figs, tomatoes and apples, turmeric, ginger, vanilla, saffron, radish, nutmeg, paprika, juniper, cinnamon, cardamom, sesame, poppy, coriander, mint, hibiscus tea, tabasco, soy sauce, curry and a good selection of vinegars, oils, grappas and wines. This is the only place where tea lovers are guaranteed to find fresh, loose-leaf tea.

CURRY

OREGANO

WHITE PEPPER

CLOVES

_29

DRIED GINGER

NUTMEG

Wan Xin Store ▶ E

Santa Croce 155, Fondamenta Minotto, +39 041 710264 open all week (9 am–7.30 pm)

A Chinese store that sells mushrooms as well as spices, excellent tofu, rice flour, red seaweed, agar agar, pasta for spring rolls, bizarre-looking frozen fish, rice and tinned foods from all around the world. Much frequented by the flourishing, if little-seen, Chinese community.

Matisse ▶ H

San Polo 53, Sotoportego de Rialto, +39 041 2770799, closed Sunday (10.30 am–7.30 pm)

A vast range of stunningly beautiful candles with leaves, coffee beans, cinnamon or dried fruit.
Some are really sculptures or bas reliefs, but don't be afraid to light them.
They're made with palm oil which, unlike paraffin, does not drip unevenly.
Above all, it is more healthful. The ones containing essences are also used for aroma therapy.

fruit and vegetables

«Here Rialto looks like a garden, so many are the herbs brought from nearby places» was how Marin Sanudo described the Rialto market in the 16th century. There were many water-level gardens and orchards on the islands in the lagoon and on the sandy shores around it. From Chioggia, Malamocco, Pellestrina, Sant'Erasmo, Mazzorbo, Vignole, Torcello, Cavallino and Lio Piccolo there came *caorlina* boats laden with lettuce, cauliflower, head lettuce, green asparagus, peas, string beans, fennel, spinach, egg plants and artichokes. Often, they plied the canals and sold their wares door to door from the water. Even today, there are still two "floating greengrocers", one at the end of Via Garibaldi at Castello and the other at the Ponte dei Pugni between Campo San Barnaba and Santa Margherita.

However, most of the boats unload at the Rialto *erbaria*, the open air market that has been doing business for more than eight centuries. Vegetables from the estuary jostle for space with products from the general markets. The *frutariòl* bawls out the incomparable virtues of locally grown *sparasèle* and *castraùre*.

The lagoon-grown purple artichoke, tender and fleshy thanks to the islands' local climate and sandy, muddy soil, is as good as any you can find. The tender, chewy *carciofo di Sant'Erasmo* (Saint Erasmus' artichoke) is prickly and elongated in shape, with dark purple leaves. At Venice, the artichoke season starts in late April, when the *castraùre* are cut. These are the first, very tender tips, which are removed to encourage the growth of the other shoots. Then it is the turn of the young plants, and finally of the more mature artichokes, which are picked in the second half of June. The Rialto market is open every morning from Tuesday to Saturday, as are the market in Rio Terà San Leonardo and the stalls in Campo Santa Margherita.

àmolo damson

armelìn apricot

articiòco artichoke (June), see also *fondi* and *castraùre*

bagìgi peanuts

bisi peas (June-July) *rìsi e bìsi* is the thick rice soup made with peas and a delicately flavoured stock obtained from the pods; in the past, some recipes included fennel seeds as a flavouring

bruscàndoli wild hop buds used in risottos and other dishes (April)

carletti wild herb used to flavour risottos and omelettes (March-May)

castraùre the tips of the artichoke's first shoots, which can been eaten raw, cooked with oil and garlic, or fried in batter

erbète rave beetroot

fasiòli beans, a crucial ingredient in *pasta e fasiòli* (pasta and beans)

fenòci fennel

fondi larger artichokes are trimmed of their stem and leaves, leaving the *fondo* or bottom. These can be cooked in a *tècia* (low-sided saucepan), first with oil and garlic, then with a little water

narànsa orange

parsèmolo parsley

pèrsego peach

pevaroni bell peppers

pòmi apple

pomidori tomatoes

sarèsa cherry

sègola onion, a basic ingredient in the preparation of many recipes, from *bigoli in salsa* (thick pasta in anchovy sauce) to *sardèle in saòr* (sardines in marinade) to Venetian-style liver

stracaganàse dried chestnuts (the name means "jaw-strainers")

spàresi asparagus

sparesèle wild asparagus (May-June)

spezzati dried peas that have split in two during dehydration

sùca pumpkin

suchete baby marrows or zucchini (May-September)

tegoline string beans (July-September), traditionally stewed or boiled

✾ plants and flowers

Venice is a city that uses stone to conceal its gardens large and small. Those who are not fortunate enough to own a garden are reduced to walking beneath red brick walls, their noses in the air to catch the fragrances of invisible wistaria, jasmine or roses. Luckily, there are florists who enable the garden-deprived to grace their homes or balconies with a plant or a bunch of flowers.

Saint Mark levels the playing field. On his feast day, 25 April, it is the Venetian custom to give women young or old, rich or poor, a *bòcolo*, a red rosebud. There are flower stalls every Tuesday and Saturday in the Rialto market, in Campo Santa Margherita, in Campo Santa Maria Formosa and Campo Santa Maria del Giglio.

BÓCOLO

32_

San Rocco ▶ H

San Polo 3127, Campiello San Rocco, +39 041 5244271, closed Sunday afternoon (8.30 am–12.30 pm and 3.30 pm–7.30 pm)
Popular with students, who buy laurel wreaths for graduation day and fresh flowers the rest of the year.

Fantin ▶ H

San Marco 4805, Campo San Salvador, +39 041 5226808, +39 041 5238479, closed Wednesday afternoon and on Sunday only in summer (8 am–12.30 pm and 3 pm–7.30 pm)
Very central, well stocked and blessed with professional staff. Good selection of bonsai, orchids of all kinds, peonies, zamias, dracaenas, liconias and unusual ginger flowers.

San Marco ▶ G

San Marco 3741, Calle della Mandola, +39 041 5228583, closed Sunday (8.30 am–12.45 pm and 3 pm–7.30 pm)
Giorgio and Sergio decorate half of Venice's palazzos. They offer a huge range of orchids and lilium, as well as garden and indoor plants.

La Dogaressa ▶G

San Polo 1756, Campo San Cassian, +39 041 5208517, closed Wednesday and Sunday (9.30 am–1 pm and 3.30 pm–7 pm)

A good selection and good prices. Indoor and outdoor plants, superb bouquets and green arrangements.

Biancat ▶G

San Polo 1474, Campiello dei Meloni, +39 041 5206522, closed Wednesday afternoon and Sunday (8.30 am–1 pm and 3.30 pm–7.30 pm)

A favourite with elegant ladies in search of sophisticated flower arrangements or exclusive statice, lysianthus or roses.

Laguna Fiorita ▶C

Cannaregio 3546, Fondamenta dell'Abazia, +39 041 5244097, closed Saturday afternoon and Sunday (8.30 am–12.30 pm and 2.30 pm–5 pm)

Venice's only city-centre nursery. Laguna Fiorita is a co-operative set up by a group of likeable green-fingered youngsters who wanted to offer a route into the job market for ten differently able workers. The dazzling, brightly coloured, 350 square-metre space offers garden plants

(hydrangeas, roses, hedge plants), indoor plants (geraniums of all kinds, or cheerful cyclamens) and a fine selection of herbs, from rosemary to thyme, marjoram and more. Laguna Fiorita also designs and looks after gardens, terraces and *altane*, the characteristic wooden Venetian roof gardens.

fish and shellfish

At the Rialto *pescaria*, the fish market, there is always a wide choice of seafood from the lagoon and Adriatic Sea. Since the Middle Ages, fish has had pride of place on the Venetian table, particularly among the less well-off. The menu includes brill, sea bream, *barboni*, *bisati*, pike, tench, *cievoli* (grey mullet), *lotregàni* (young grey mullet), *volpine* (three-year-old grey mullet) and *boseghe*, *gò*, bass, *asià*, *raze* (skate), *passerini* (flounders), *sfogi* (plaice) and mackerel. And of course the ubiquitous *sardèle* and *sardoni*. Shellfish and molluscs include crab of all kinds – *granzi, mazanete, moleche – schìe*, *scampi*, lobster, cuttlefish, squid, *granzipòri*, *granzeole*, *peoci*, *pevarasse*, *caparossoli*, *cape longhe*, *cape tonde*, *canoce* and

FAN SHELL SCALLOPS

34– *capesante*. As well as being fried, boiled, baked or grilled, fish can be served, depending on type, in *brodeto* (soup), *sguazzetto* (stew), *casso pipa* (cooked in an earthenware pot with a lid), *in saòr* (marinade) or *alla busara* (cooked in hot oil, garlic, pepper, white wine and breadcrumbs, then browned in the oven). The mouthwatering *molèche col pien* are soft-shell crabs that are placed alive in beaten egg and parmesan. When they have eaten their fill, they are dusted in flour and fried.

MANTIS PRAWNS

| JOHN DORY | SEA SNAILS | RED MULLET | ANCHOVIES |

| SARDINES | LATI DE SEPIA | CUTTLEFISH | ZÒTOLI |

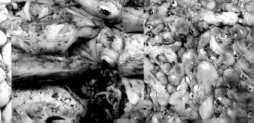

anguèla sand smelt, a small, common lagoon-dwelling fish, also called *acquadella*

asià spiny dogfish

àstese common lobster

baccalà mantecato boiled stockfish, flaked then steamed and aromatised with garlic and parsley; it is then blended with oil, like a mayonnaise, until creamy

baìcolo the young sea bass

barbòn red mullet (September-November)

bevarasse cockles or clams (all year round)

bisàto adult eel (August-November)

bòsega grey mullet (September-October)

bovolèto edible snail, boiled and served as a *cicheto* with garlic and parsley

branzino bass, a much prized species of fish (July-December)

calamaretto baby squid (September-October)

canestrello small scallop (September-October)

canòce mantis prawn (September-November)

capalònga or **càpa da dèo** razor shell (September-October)

caparòssolo cross-cut carpet shell, or *vongola verace* in Italian (all year round)

capasanta fan shell scallop, Saint James' shell, or in French "coquilles Saint-Jacques"; Venetian scallops are smaller and tastier (October-November)

càpatonda or **margaròta** a bivalve mollusc found on the lagoon bed and sandbars

caragòl generic name for various species of winkle-like molluscs with pointed, helical shells; changing environmental conditions have caused a dramatic fall in their numbers

corbo de sasso corb or brown meagre (April-September)

folpo common octopus, with two rows of suckers on the tentacles

folpetto or *moscardino* octopus with a single row of suckers on the tentacles

gamberetto shrimp (November-February)

garùsolo sea snail, served as an appetiser; they are extracted from the shell with a toothpick and eaten fresh (June-September)

gò goby (October-March)

gransèola spiny spider crab; the carapace can be as large as 20 cm across (October-December); it is boiled, cleaned and dressed with oil, garlic, parsley and lemon; the flesh is then reinserted into the shell and served

grànso edible crab or common shore crab; commonly found in the lagoon, it is called *masanèta*, *spiàntano* or *moèca*, depending on its stage of development

late de sepia (literally "cuttlefish milk") contents of cuttlefish egg or sperm sac

masanèta female crab (October-November), particularly sought after when it is carrying eggs

molèca male *masanèta*, caught during the moulting period when the shell is soft and the crabs can be eaten whole (March-April and October-November)

mormora sea bream (April-September)

novellàme name used for the fry of sea fish only; the term derives from *novèllo*, meaning "young"

oràda gilthead bream (July-September)

oradèlla or **oradìna** immature gilthead bream

passarìn small plaice (September-November)

peòcio mussel (June-September)

pessenovèllo another name for novellàme

San Pietro John Dory (all year round)

sardèla sardine (June-October). In the well-known Venetian specialty *sardèle in saòr*, sardines are dusted in flour and fried, then marinaded with sliced onions and slowly fried with vinegar, pine nuts and sultanas; heavenly!

sardon anchovy (June-October)

schìa small grey shrimp, much prized and very common in the lagoon; usually, they are shelled, boiled and dressed, or cooked in a sauce, to be served with polenta, but they can also be fried (October-December)

s-ciòso snail

sèpa cuttlefish, traditionally cooked in its ink, is served with polenta or as a sauce for risottos or pasta (July-August)

sfògio sole (August-October)

soàso brill (October)

zòtolo small cuttlefish

MOLÉCA

 # cheese

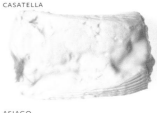

Venetians tend to prefer cheeses and cold meats
from the former mainland protectorates of the Most
Serene Republic. The Colli Berici and Colli Euganei
provide mature hams guaranteed by consortia.
From the hills and countryside of Treviso come Piave
caciottina, Montella *casatella* and Combai *ricotta*
cheeses, salami, pressed meats and sausages.
Cansiglio supplies mountain dairy cheese and
smoked ricotta. The Asiago tableland yields the much
sought-after fresh or mature Asiago cheese and the
valleys of Trentino provide *Vezzena*, one of Italy's
finest cheeses. Finally, Friuli provides Montasio and
36– Carnia cheeses, and DOC products from the Carnian
Alps and Pre-Alps, but then Venetians have always
been partial to anything *furlàn*.

ASIAGO

Aliani ▶ G
San Polo 654, Ruga Rialto, +39 041 5224913,
closed Sunday and Monday afternoon (8 am–1 pm and 5 pm–7.30 pm)

Venice's most famous delicatessen. Busy mums, and lazy but
discriminating singles, snap up the ready-made *pasticcio di
lasagne* with meat, vegetables or fish sauce, turkey with tuna,
roast meat and potatoes, cuttlefish cooked in their ink with
polenta, or rabbit with honey fungus. There's a great selection
of fresh and mature cheeses, as well as cold meats.
Choose from Sauris ham, horsemeat bresaola, Treviso casatella
cheese, mascarpone, Castelmagno, red wine-soaked Ubriaco
cheese, truffle-aromatised Sottocenere al Tartufo cheese and the
celebrated cheeses of Friuli. This is just the place to buy some
good local cheese before leaving Venice. They'll even vacuum-
pack it for you.

MONTASIO MEZZANO

VEZZENA

MATURE ASIAGO

PICKLED VENETO CHILLI PEPPERS

La Baita ►H

San Polo 47, Ruga degli Oresi, +39 041 5236906, closed Wednesday
afternoon and Sunday (8 am–1 pm and 4.30 pm–7 pm)

In their tiny two square-metre stall wedged into
a portico, three super-efficient assistants serve up
food products, entertaining banter and shameless
flattery. Their buffalo mozzarella, casatella and
stracchino cheeses are always fresh, the sliced
meats are good and the mature cheeses are well
up to snuff. But don't try to jump the queue!

Casa del Parmigiano ►H

San Polo 214, Campo della Bella Vienna, +39 041 5206525, closed Sunday and afternoons from
Monday to Thursday (8 am–1 pm and 4.30 pm–7.30 pm)

The windows look onto a well-ventilated *campo* that was once packed with
fruit stalls. You might hear a polite "*mi scusi, ma c'ero prima io*" (excuse
me, I was first), but when it is your turn, try the soft cheeses. Fresh buffalo
mozzarella, *burrata*, mascarpone and creamy ricotta may not be good for
your waistline, but they are good enough to enjoy as a dessert.

Lorenzo ►H

San Marco 4666, Calle dei Fabbri, +39 041 5232682, closed Wednesday afternoon and Sunday
(7.30 am–1.30 pm and 4.30 pm–8.30 pm)

This very central shop is much
frequented by well-dressed clients
attracted by the cornucopia of
French, British and craft-made Italian delicacies. The jars of sauces, oils,
preserves, honey, honey, jam and caviar are impressive, but the carefully
selected cold meats and cheeses are even better. The meats include air-
cured prosciutto crudo ham from Parma, San Daniele, the Veneto and
Tuscany, culatello di zibello, stroglino and salame gentile. Among the
cheeses are cacio, caciocavallo and provolone from Irpinia, cave-matured
pecorino di fossa and the unmissable Verde di Montegalda.

Bianchi ►Q

Castello 1561, Via Garibaldi, +39 041 5221156, closed Wednesday afternoon
and Sunday (7.30 am–1 pm and 4.30 pm–7.30 pm)

Sometimes you see magnificent yachts moored at Riva dei Sette Martiri.

A young crew member
might come ashore, stride
purposefully towards Via
Garibaldi, then duck into
what looks like any other *biavaiòl*, or neighbourhood store. It
even has the local kids' drawings on the wall. But Bianchi is
where for the past three decades Gabriele has been attracting
a gourmet clientele, A-list celebs included, to Venice's least
pretentious district with Bitto, Castelmagno, Stilton, Buche
and mountain dairy taleggio, not to mention great hillside
Parmesan cheese matured for 30 months. There's also
swordfish, tuna, breast of goose, Jolanda De Colò's turkey
filetto and, at Christmastime, fillet of sturgeon.

meats and cold meats

SOPPRESSA PRESSED MEAT

SALAMI

The lagoon supplies *selvadego de val* (game), in the shape of *masorini, foleghe, salsegne* or *alzavole* (teal), *ciossi* or *fischioni* (widgeon), *pignoli* or *canapiglie* (gadwall), to be made into ragout or elaborate, spice-rich sweet and sour sauces. Even today, the *beccherie* (butcher's shops) put out a sign in November that says *xe rivà el castrà* to announce the arrival of salted, smoked and sun-dried wether mutton. Today, the mutton is salted, smoked gigot of lamb, which is more tender and has a less pungent flavour. *Castradina* in broth *co le verze* (with cabbage) is the traditional dish for the feast of the Madonna della Salute (Presentation of Mary), on 21 November. The art of preparing sophisticated recipes from offal is being lost. There is less call

OSSOCOLLO

38— nowadays for *spiensa* (spleen), *fongadina* or *coradea* (mixed offal), not to mention *potacelo de testina* (pig's head).

ànara duck (October-November)

barbunsàl calf's chin, boiled with carrots and celery, then dressed with oil and vinegar when cold

bechèr butcher

castrà wether mutton, the meat of a castrated ram; *castradìna* (spiced smoked leg) is traditionally served with cabbage on the feast of the Madonna della Salute

cren horseradish sauce, served with boiled meats

dìndio turkey

durèlo chicken gizzard

figà liver; *figà a la venexiàna* is thinly sliced calf's liver cooked over a low flame with onions

folega coot; when the birds ate only fish, their meat acquired an unpleasant flavour; now that they are farmed and eat feed, they have become a delicacy

lièvaro hare

luganega long fresh pork sausage, served with rice (*risi*)

masorin (October-November) male duck; should not weigh more than one kilogram

musetto a pork sausage similar to cotechino but made mainly with meat from the *muso* (head), steamed or boiled; it is served sliced with potato purée and lentils

nervetti veal cartilage boiled and served as *cicheti* (bar snacks), with onion, parsley, vinegar and oil

osei scampài (literally, "birds that got away"); skewers of veal, beef or pork with lard, sage and white wine; the name derives from the Venetian habit of serving small birds roasted on a skewer

ossocollo coppa sausage

polastro chicken, also a name for an ingenuous or silly person

rumegàl calf's gullet

sangueto black pudding made from pig's blood cooked with onion and other flavourings until thick enough to be sliced

sècoe the small pieces of flesh that remain attached to the spine of the cow or calf; used mainly in risottos, they were once the food of the poor but can now be found even in the best restaurants

sòpa coàda soup made of bread and roast pigeon

spiènsa spleen

tetina cow's udder

vedèlo calf

LUGANEGA

Battistin Caroldi ► H

San Marco 4676, Calle dei Fabbri, +39 041 5230547, closed Sunday (7 am–1 pm)

Popular with fans of fiorentina (T-bone) steaks and the like.

Biancon ► H

San Polo 203, Casaria, +39 041 5227840, closed Sunday (7 am–1 pm)

Mainly horsemeat, available as steaks, hamburgers, stewing steak,
mince, dried and salted bresaola, salami and ham.

Boutique della Carne ► A

Cannaregio 1373, Rio Terà San Leonardo, +39 041 718567, closed Monday and Wednesday (7
am–1 pm and 4 pm–7.30 pm)

Despite the cringeworthy name ("Meat Boutique"), this is a good
place to come for Chianina beef and other Tuscan products, including
a small selection of cheeses and salamis. There's also Argentine beef,
French chicken, suckling pig, entrecôte steaks, American and Canadian bison,
bison salami, kosher beef sausage, Abruzzo lamb and reindeer, if you order in advance.

Cappon ► I

Castello 5223, Calle Lunga Santa Maria Formosa,
+39 041 5224053, closed Sunday (7.30 am–1 pm,
Friday and Saturday also open 4 pm–7.30 pm)

Cappon owes part of its success to the busy
mums who come here for the ready-to-cook
meatballs, meat loaves, cutlets, veal and ham
saltimbocca and roulades.

Giacomin ► G

San Marco 3710, Calle della Mandola, +39 041 5226376,
closed Sunday (8 am–1.30 pm)

Kid and lamb from Sardinia and Tuscany,
pressed meats from Friuli, as well as excellent
pancetta (bacon) and slightly smoked guanciale
(pork jowl). The ready to cook stuffed rabbit
legs and roast beef are handy in an emergency.
Occasionally, you can find craft-made butter from
Carnia. Look out for it!

Zamattio ► F

Dorsoduro 3930, Calle de la Dona Onesta, +39 041 5237969, closed Sunday (7 am–2 pm, Friday and Saturday also open 4 pm–8 pm)

Boned and stuffed rabbit and guinea fowl, as well as excellent cold meats including air-cured Parma
prosciutto crudo ham, matured for 22 months.

Laguna Carni ► G

San Polo 315, Ruga dei Spezieri, +39 041 5223232,
closed Sunday (7 am–1.30 pm)

If you want to try your hand at traditional
recipes, this is where you will find
the celebrated *trippa rissa* tripe and,
in season, game from the lagoon.

wines and spirits

Since cellars are out of the question in Venice, it is difficult to lay down serious wines.

Unless you have a climate-conditioned room, you'll have to drink your wines soon after purchase.

Bàcari was the name for shops that sold Puglian wines, and *malvasie* retailed the equivalent product from Istria. Their thirst quenched, patrons could then visit a *fritolìn* for a snack of fried whitebait.

Nowadays, palates are more refined so Venetians go to an enoteca (wine shop) to buy, or be recommended, the right bottle. Most still drink *spritz* as an aperitif, *sgropìn* (sorbet of lemon, vodka and prosecco wine) at the end of a fish-based meal and *torbolìn* (very young, sweetish, slightly cloudy wine) after dinner in late autumn.

Spritz is Venice's most popular aperitif. The name recalls a habit of the Austrian soldiers who occupied the city from 1814 to 1866. They found Italian wines too alcoholic, so they diluted them with water (*spritzen* means "to splash" in German). Today, the ingredients are four parts white wine, three parts sparkling mineral water or better still soda water, two parts Select, Campari or Aperol and a piece of lemon rind.

Every bar professional has his or her own personal recipe and proportions, but don't worry too much about the alcohol content. You're unlikely to be driving anywhere.

Cantinone – formerly Schiavi ▶ N

Dorsoduro 992, Ponte San Trovaso, +39 041 5230034, closed Sunday afternoon (8.30 am–8.30 pm)

The traditional place for an *ombrèta* (small glass of wine) and one of Alessandra's creative canapés, such as tartare sauce and plain chocolate, tuna sauce and thinly sliced leek, or walnut sauce with ricotta and currants. There's also an entire wall to muse over as you select a bottle of Prosecco, Cabernet, Amarone, grappa or whisky. Alessandra has something for all budgets.

Bottiglieria Colonna ▶ H

Castello 5595, Castello della Fava, +39 041 5285137, closed Sunday (9 am–1 pm and 4 pm–8 pm)

The wines here are mainly from Veneto, Friuli and Tuscany. There's a good range of spirits, including whisky, grappa, cognac and gin for promoting a party mood. The home delivery service is a godsend.

Vino e... vini ▶ L

Castello 3301, Fondamenta dei Furlani, +39 041 5210184, closed Sunday (9 am–1 pm and 5 pm–8 pm)

Enrico is in charge here. He has a good selection of middle to top-of-the-range wines, plus about 90 grappas from all over Italy. They go from Frescobaldi's *La Luce* to peatier versions and the fragrant December grappas. Then there are cognacs, calvados, armagnacs, brandies and meditation wines like Torcolato, Sauternes or dried-grape passito. Enrico keeps about 60 of the best champagnes and 40 or so balsamic vinegars. He also has a small selection of other delights, including paté and chocolate.

Millevini ►H

San Marco 5362, Ramo del Fontego dei Turchi, +39 041 5206090, closed Sunday (10.30 am–8.15 pm)

This enoteca (wine shop) only opened recently, hence the modern decor. In addition to the "thousand wines" (mille vini) of the sign over the door – you'll see bottles of still and sparkling stuff from France, California and Spain – visitors can pick up whisky, grappa, preserves, sauces, oils and balsamic vinegars, not to mention excellent abbey-brewed beers.

Alla Botte ►H

San Marco 5529, Calle della Bissa, +39 041 2960596, closed Sunday (10 am–1 pm and 4 pm–8 pm)

Good range of premium wines, grappas and craft beers, but many people come here for the red and white wines from Treviso and Friuli, sold unbottled.

Here are one or two places where you nibble a *cicheto* (bar snack) with your wine.

Aciugheta ►I

Castello 4357, Campo Santi Filippo e Giacomo, +39 041 5224292, open all week (9 am–12 pm)

For some time, this bar and pizzeria has been famous for its great spread of *cicheti* (bar snacks) and wines by the glass. Now, they have added some excellent bottles and interesting gourmet foods to the list. If you need any help, ask for Gianni.

Mascareta ►I

Castello 5183, Calle Lunga Santa Maria Formosa, +39 041 5230744, closed Wednesday and Thursday (7 pm–2 am)

The irrepressible Mauro Lorenzon, inventor and president of Enoiteche, is now ensconced here at Mascareta. So if you're looking for a bottle from his superb selection, you'll have to resign yourself to doing some tasting. Mauro has still wines, spumante, grappas, salami, cheese, a small but very exclusive kitchen. And oysters!

Al Prosecco ►F

Santa Croce 1503, San Giacomo dall'Orio, +39 041 5240222, closed Sunday (8 am–8.30 pm)

Another place with great wine, mainly from the Triveneto regions. Taste them with a selection of salami and cheeses in the intimate dining room, or at a table in the breezy, lively *campo* outside.

 # clothing and accessories

Once upon a time, Venice was the capital of European fashion.
The city manufactured and imported sumptuous materials, from two-pile velvet
to satin and brocades woven with gold or silver thread, as well as precious stones.
Semi-precious stones were also in demand, for there was a thriving business in
glass-paste imitations for jewellery. Sophisticated, if often over-the-top, luxury
was the order of the day. Venetian women were famed for their elegance,
glamour and audacious taste in colour.

The shops and emporia, fabric retailers, *oresi* (goldsmiths), *sartori* (tailors) and *baretèri* (hatters) catered for every need. Today, creativity and eccentricity are still very much in evidence, especially in clothing accessories.

42_

Longo ▶H

San Marco 4813, Calle del Lovo, +39 041 5226454, closed Sunday (9.30 am–7.30 pm)

A milliner's. One of Giuliana's many virtues is that she has
rediscovered the traditional gondolier's winter hat, the black
cloth article with the pompom. She is also the vice chair
of the *El Fèlze* association (see p. 100).

The workroom at this very central shop produces made-to-
measure or personalised women's hats in straw, fabric or felt,
original Doge's *zoggia* headgear and flamboyant decorated
cocked hats for Carnival or fancy-dress parties.

If you are lucky enough to own a vintage aeroplane
or motor car, you will enjoy her period costumes,
including Lindbergh's jacket, Fangio's trousers
and 1950s flying jackets, complete
with helmet and goggles.

Finally, Giuliana has Venice's finest
selection of Panamas, the famous
Ecuadorian hats affected by so
many fashion-conscious celebs.

Bellinaso ►G

San Polo 1226, Campo Sant'Aponal,
+39 041 5223351, closed Sunday (10
am–1.30 pm and 3 pm–7 pm)

A fine array of brightly
coloured scarves, gloves,
hemp (€ 110-200) or straw
(€ 250-450) hats, jackets,
bags (€ 90-170) and
slipper-shoes (€ 70-95) in
a thousand different
shades and shapes,
all elegantly basic.

La Fenice Atelier ►○

San Marco 3537, Ponte dei Frati, +39 041 5230578, closed Sunday (10.30 am–7.30 am)

Cristina Linassi offers fairy-tale lingerie in pure white hand-
embroidered linen with a 19th-century flavour, sheets and pillowcases
with hemstitching or satin stitch designs, tablecloths and napkins.
Many of the sophisticated fabrics are made to order from silk, linen,
cotton, damask or cotton satin in ivory, golden yellow or sage green.

Araba Fenice ►○

San Marco 1822, Calle dei Barcaroli, +39 041
5220664, closed Sunday (9.30 am–7.30 pm)

Loris is a much-admired
designer who disapproves of big-
name labels. He does appreciate
leading-edge styling and quality
in cutting and materials, often
linen, wool crepe or wool and
viscose. He also enjoys creating
necklaces from rock crystal, onyx
and coral, and makes interesting
lamps.

The **tabarro** is a billowing winter cape in heavy cloth of spun but not carded wool. The fabric is so closely woven that after cutting it does not need to be edged to prevent it unravelling. It comprises six metres of fabric with a single seam along the back. In Venice the silk, hooded *dòmino* version was particularly popular. Black, heavy and reaching down to the ankles, it was a favourite with 18th-century noblemen and women who wished to conceal the sumptuous, and severely prohibited, elegance of their clothes and jewellery. The *dòmino* ensured discretion, enabling its wearers to sin in safety without fear of discovery. In the 20th century, the *tabarro* was replaced by the more practical overcoat, and continued to be worn only in the countryside and smaller villages. Today, it is not unusual to come across *tabarro*-toting locals who add an extra touch of picturesqueness to an already scenic cityscape.

Balocoloc ▶ G

Santa Croce 2134, Calle Longa, +39 041 5240551, closed Sunday and Monday (9 am–5 pm)

It may not be much to look at, but this craft workshop is the place to come for traditional gondolier's outfits. Carnival costumes, heavy cloaks (€ 250-350), lighter walking cloaks and a fine selection of well-made, attractively priced (€ 30-180) women's headgear are all waiting.

Store ▶ H

San Marco 4260b, Campo San Luca, +39 041 5238457, closed Sunday
(9.30 am–12.30 pm and 3.30 pm–8 pm)

This is where the Venetians who matter come for a jacket that proves the point. Nicola Grillo gets his stock from all over Europe. Tailored garments come from Arnys in Paris, five-pocket golfing trousers and leather braces are from Pepe Mateu in Barcelona, hats come from Britain, original polo wear from Argentina, jackets and other items used by the buttero cowboys from Maremma in Tuscany, leather Felisi bags and suitcases from Ferrara, as well as clothing from the Antico Sartoria di Maremma, Barbour, Jeckerson and La Martina.
This is also the sole outlet in Venice for the Tabarrificio Veneto's historically accurate traditional cloaks. Choose from *nobiluomo, brigantino, lustrissimo, ruzzante, mercante padano* and other styles.

Ikat ▸G

San Polo 1727, Calle dei Cristi,
+39 041 5242690, closed
Monday and Wednesday
mornings (10.30 am–12.30 pm
and 4.30 pm–7.30 pm)

The general ambience
is ethnic, but if you take
a closer look at the many
things Mariolina and
Daniela bring back from
their trips round the world,
you'll see some items they have
made themselves. These include necklaces (€ 50-
200), bracelets and comfortable ballerina-style
deerskin shoes (€ 93), as well as slightly odd but
excellent-quality scarves and shawls. Much loved by
well-travelled women who know their way around.

—45

Godi Fiorenza ▸H

San Marco 4261, Campo San Luca,
+39 041 2410866, closed Sunday
(10 am–12.30 pm and 3.30 pm–7.30 pm)

Sisters Patrizia and Samanta were born in Venice, but have
lived and studied in London.
This dual background comes out in their creations. They
combine superb
traditional tailoring with a modern take, so their elaborate but
eminently wearable range can be matched with casual items.
For example, the embroidered corsets (€ 270) are available
made to measure. The duo also make very unusual necklaces.

Hibiscus ▸G

San Polo 1061, Rughetta del Ravano, +39 041 5208989,
open all week (9.30 am–7.30 pm, Sunday opening from 11 am)

Feminine ethnochic. Lovely jackets, stoles and coloured
scarves in linen, cotton, silk and other natural fibres. Each
item is a one-off creation by a Venetian designer.
Costume jewellery by Maria Calderara. The clientele is radical,
sophisticated and very well heeled.

Camiceria San Marco ►○

San Marco 1340, Calle Vallaresso, +39 041 5221432, closed Sunday (9.30 am–7.30 pm)

Men's and women's made-to-measure shirts (€ 175-280). You can take
your own dream shirt in to be copied, or choose from the 40 or so models and 200 types of fabric,
including cotton, silk, linen and wool for Chanel-type suits (€ 1350). Your shirt will be ready in ten days.

Banco N. 10 ►L

Castello 3478, Salizada Sant'Antonin, +39 041 5221439, closed Sunday and
Monday (10 am–1 pm and 4 pm–7.30 pm)

The clothes here are made by detainees at the Giudecca
women's prison. The jackets (€ 80-140) and bags (€ 30-
80) are classic, and occasionally tongue-in-cheek. They
are beautifully made with fine-quality textiles – including
upholstery fabrics – which the prison manages to obtain
at knockdown prices. But there are also brocades,
velvets, silk and linen, ready-to-wear or made-to-
measure (delivery will take a fortnight). Well
worth a visit.

L'Angolo ►M

Dorsoduro 2755, Calle Lunga San Barnaba, +39 041 2777895, closed Sunday (10.30 am–1 pm
and 4 pm–7.30 pm)

Cristina Albertini makes colourful and very practical two-tone cotton
bags (€ 50), as well as unusual wrist bags (€ 30) for those evenings
when you need somewhere to keep your mobile, your keys and not
much else. You'll also see bigger velvet bags printed in exclusive
patterns by
the Minelli
sisters.

Mazzon — Le Borse ▶F

San Polo 2807, Campiello San Tomà, +39 041 5203421, closed Sunday (9 am–12.30 pm and 3.30 pm–7.30 pm)

Word of mouth has made Mazzon famous with the well-to-do ladies of Italy's rich north east. The leather is superb and the details professional, which means you can pick up a designer-quality bag at affordable prices (€ 85-250). There's a vast range of styles and about 30 colours, so you're sure to find what you're looking for.

Il Grifone ▶E

Dorsoduro 3516, Fondamenta del Gaffaro, +39 041 5229452, closed Sunday and Monday (10 am–1 pm and 6 pm–7.30 pm)

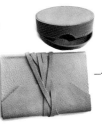

Toni Peressin makes bags, briefcases, backpacks (€ 75-120), purses, notebooks, pouches and cases in leather and chamois leather. The "Bertinotti" neck purse (€ 20), has achieved legendary status with students at the nearby Faculty of Architecture, who have nicknamed it after an Italian politician who sports a distinctive neck-hung glasses case.

–47

Margerie ▶O

San Marco 2511b, Campiello della Feltrina, +39 041 5236393, closed Sunday (10 am–1 pm and 2.30 pm–7.30 pm)

The chirpy young woman who greets you as you enter this fairy-tale shop – with a real rabbit – is Margherita, the creator of everything you see. Her ideas are fresh and spontaneous. The appealing, colourful bags (€ 120-450) come in fabric or leather traditional or tote styles, studded, inlaid or decorated with pearls, flowers or cross-stitch embroidery.

Shanti Daan ▶ M

Dorsoduro 3284, Calle del Fabro, +39 041 2411916, closed Sunday (10 am–12.30 pm and 3.30 pm–7.30 pm)

Everything here is imported from India. The teak or rosewood drawer and corner units are attractive and affordable. Among all the clothes, bags, jewellery and puppets, there's also a collection of small Ganeshes. But what's a rickshaw doing in the centre of Venice?

Mistero Atelier ▶ I

Castello 4925, Ruga Giuffa, +39 041 5227797, open all week (9.30 am–1.30 pm and 3.30 pm-7.30 pm)

The bags, jackets and trousers are made in-house, but the main attraction is the range of scarves (€13-20) and shawls (€ 25-50) that come in 360 shades. Made from raw silk, linen, shimmering shantung or taffeta, they are imported from India, Thailand, Laos and Cambodia. The silver jewellery with silk inset is out of the ordinary (€ 25-200).

Crovato ▶ N

San Marco 2995, Calle delle Botteghe, +39 041 5204170, closed Sunday and Monday morning (11 am–1 pm and 4 pm–7.30 pm)

A magnet for rhinestone cowgirls. More than one high-society lady has turned to Laura for help with something to wear to a particularly challenging event. Eyebrow-raising evening wear (€ 40) is her forte, but patient shoppers can find great, if slightly crumpled, bargains in the baskets (€ 10-20).

Fiorella Gallery ▶N

San Marco 2806, Campo Santo Stefano, +39 041 5209228,
open Monday to Saturday and sometimes on Sunday (10
am-7.30pm)

Don't be put off by the audacity of the ever-
provocative Fiorella Mancini's stunning
showroom. A velvet or gauze kimono (€
700-1,000) might be too much for you, but
the silkscreen printed velvet jackets (€ 550)
are eminently wearable.

Elcanapon ▶G

Santa Croce 1906, Salizada San Stae, +39 041
2440247, closed Sunday and Monday (9.45 am–
1.30 pm and 4 pm–7.30 pm)

A shop with a theme. This is the place
for anything to do with Indian hemp,
and all you need to grow it.
There are jackets, trousers, skirts,
blouses (€ 70-120), sandals, clogs (€
45), scarves, bags, bits and pieces,
soap, chocolate, oil, herbal infusions,
pasta, lollipops, fertiliser, lamps,
hookahs, pipes, papers and a small
selection of radical and no-global literature.

–49

Daniele ▶G

San Polo 2235, Calle Scaleter, +39 041 5246242, closed Sunday (10 am–12.30 pm, 3 pm–6.30 pm and 9.30 pm–12.00 pm)

Monica Daniele can show you women's and men's hats, *tabarro* cloaks (€ 300-1,000), traditional
shawls and made-to-measure historic costumes. In among the cloaks and hats is a small publisher.
One of Albert Gardin's latest efforts is a translation of Homer's Iliad into Venetian!

👓 eyewear

Venice was where the world's first eyeglasses were made, at the same time as the Chinese were discovering them in the 13th century. The two transparent pieces of glass were held together by a nail. In the early days, anyone who dared to reveal how they were made risked the death penalty.

Later on, ever more sophisticated frames and lens shapes appeared. There was even a curious version that could be hooked onto a wig or hat. In the 18th century, Venice was also the setting for the invention of that elegant eyewear item, the pince-nez.

Micromega ▶○

San Marco 2436, Calle de le Ostreghe, +39 041 2960765,
open all week (10 am–7.30 pm, Sunday 11 am–7 pm)

This is the place to come for the world's lightest glasses with a frame that weighs less than one gram. Owner Roberto Carlon holds the patent. The lenses are mounted without screws. In fact they are almost sewn into place, and the very flexible high-tension beta titanium structure has no critical breaking points. This enables the thickness of the lenses to be reduced to a minimum. The results

are a surprisingly comfortable fit and great stability. The various models can be personalised in endless ways with, for example, a titanium (€ 290), titanium and buffalo horn (€ 350) or 14-carat gold (€ 650) frame. Your super-light glasses will be ready in a week.

Ceccon ▶ı

Cannaregio 6420, Calle de le Erbe, +39 340 5073427, closed Sunday (2.30 pm–7.30 pm)

It has been several years since French-born Georges decided to settle in Venice and open a workshop where he could put his considerable experience as an engineer to good use. His tools are a laser for engraving metal to two millimetres, and outstanding manual dexterity. George makes titanium eyewear frames and very lightweight earrings in the same iridescent material. He also engraves to order and can personalise signs, cutlery and other objects.

Museum Shop ▶○

Dorsoduro 701, Fondamenta Venier dei Leoni, + 39 041 2405424, closed
Tuesday (10 am–6 pm)

This is the retail outlet for the Peggy Guggenheim
Collection. As well as a selection of books on
contemporary art and the usual museum stuff, there
are reproductions of the eccentric Ms Guggenheim's
vases, sandals and other personal objects, including
her astonishing eyewear (€ 120).

Carraro ▶G

San Marco 3706, Calle della Mandola, +39 041 5204258, closed Sunday (9 am–1 pm and
3 pm–7.30 pm)

As you walk down Calle della Mandola, it is hard not to notice
this well-lit optician's. The glasses are for people who like their
eyewear to be remembered. Choose from around 20 models
with frames (€ 60-80) in satin-finish, polished or rubber-tipped
acetate.

–51

Ottico Fabbricatore ▶H

San Marco 4773, Calle del Lovo, +39 041 5225263,
closed Sunday and Monday (9.30 am–12.30 pm and 3.30 pm–7.30 pm)

A small but elegant shop with plenty of good ideas. The man of
the house designs sleek frames in American buffalo horn and
titanium (€ 450-600), and blown glass lamps, while his better half
creates stylishly shaggy bags. She also has seven simple models
for splendid made-to-measure cashmere jerseys or jackets (€
450-500). Choose from around 70 colours and expect
delivery in 20 days.

Urbani ▶○

San Marco 1280, Frezzaria, +39 041 5224140, closed Sunday and Monday morning (9.30
am–12.30 pm and 3.30 pm–7.30 pm)

Fosca and Lorenzo carry on the family optician's business in
the very centre of Venice, with a range of imaginative,
brightly coloured plastic frames (€ 90-110). The
Le Corbusier is by now a classic, and particularly
popular among architecture students with high
hopes and low vision. There are also a dozen or
so other optical, folding and even gondola-shaped
models.

shoes

Shoes have always been a Venetian fetish. They were once made with silks from the east, damasks, woven velvets or lampas woven with gold thread. Heels were high, in theory to aid walking in the muddier stretches of the *calli* (streets), but actually to encourage a seductive swaying of the hips. Shoes were fashioned in a vast range of shapes and colours. Often, the leather was camouflaged under engravings, gilt finishes or precious stones. It is impossible to talk about craft shoemaking in Venice without mentioning Rolando Segalin and his workshop in Calle dei Fuseri. Three women have also mastered the art, and each carries on the tradition in her own way. You will have to wait a couple of months if you want your shoes made to measure.

52_

Zanella ▶ H

Castello 5641, Campo San Lio, +39 041 5235500, closed Sunday (9.30 am–1 pm and 5 pm–7 pm)

Giovanna is bubbly, colourful and something of a magpie. She invents multicoloured, sculpturesque hats and exciting, exclusive foulards that the alternative set dearly loves. Above all, she makes inspiring shoes to measure (€ 350-500) and extravagant painted clogs (€ 280) that are guaranteed to make an impression.

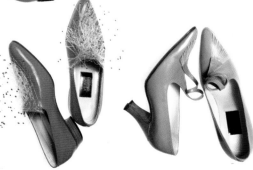

Ghezzo ▶H

San Marco 4365, Calle dei Fuseri,
+39 041 5222115, closed Sunday
(9.30 am–12.30 pm and 3.30 pm–7.30 pm)

Rolando Segalin's historic shoe
shop was acquired a few years
ago by the young but seriously
professional shoemaker, Daniela.
Made-to-measure footwear costs
from € 500 to € 850, although
crocodile can nudge the price tag
up to € 1,700. Daniela also has
reproduction 18th-century shoes
and contemporary eccentricities.
She likes soft leathers and
combining colours.

–53

Gmeiner ▶G

San Polo 951, Campiello del Sol, +39 041 5209831,
closed Saturday afternoon and Sunday
(10 am–1 pm and 2 pm–7 pm)

Gabriele Gmeiner is Austrian-born.
After studying abroad and a number
of other ventures, he opened this bright
sunny shop in the heart of the Rialto market.
Her very exclusive shoes (€ 1,200-1,500) are
all hand-sewn. Naturally, each customer has
a personal last.

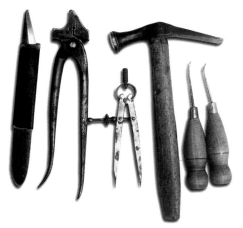

Kalimala ▸ H

Castello 5387, Salizada San Lio, +39 041 5283596, closed Sunday (9.30 am–7.30 pm)

Shoes (€ 95) and sandals (€ 80) designed in a simple, practical style and made exclusively from vegetable-cured cow leather. Gloves in lamb's leather or deerskin (€ 50-90) are on sale, with fascinating bags and belts with buckles designed in-house.

54_ ### Clinica della Scarpa ▸ G

San Polo 838a, Calle de le Do Spade, no telephone, closed Sunday and Monday (8.30 am–12.30 pm and 4 pm–6 pm)

There are still quite a few neighbourhood cobblers in Venice but Nerone Francesco Aronne Pagano is the only one who writes poetry. On the walls, the furniture, the door jamb and his apron.

Proper **scarpez** – Venetians call them *furlane* – have a sole made of part-used, two-tone bicycle tyre. The ones with fake printed-tyre soles should be shunned. In fact, this kind of footwear is a fine example of reutilisation.

The exposed chainstitch seams on the sole – which is never glued – are arranged concentrically around the edge. On the underside of the upper is a layer of jute to give the desired bulk.

Scarpez are neither shoes nor slippers. They can be worn indoors or out, and are ideal for wearing on a gondola.

They enjoyed enormous success in Venice, even among the snobbier type of local celeb, because they are strictly unisex.

Today, only a few elderly craftworkers in Friuli still make them. Since a new sole costs less than a recycled one, you'll have to keep an eye out for imitations.

Misce Pelli ▶H

Castello 6006a, Calle del Pistor, +39 041 5231356, closed Saturday afternoon and Sunday (9 am–12.25 pm and 3.30 pm–7.25 pm)

You can get a bag or shoes repaired, but this is also a shop where they'll make good copies of keys for you. They sell shoe trees or shoe stretchers, insoles, arch supports, leather laces and everything you need for your dog or cat, from pet food to toys. Don't forget the pooper-scoopers, or the fantastic gum boots for those high-water days!

Acqua alta, or "high water", is not a flood that sweeps away everything in its path. It is the slow rising of the tide – it takes six hours to flow and six to ebb – under the influence of the moon and the winds. When a particularly high tide is forecast, generally between October and December, the few shopkeepers who still suffer the effects know that they cannot leave anything on the floor. Others set up sluice gates at the entrance to their shop. When the sirens sound in the morning, that's when we get out our rubber boots.

Every self-respecting Venetian has at least two pairs. You get a slight buzz from walking, doing the shopping, or drinking a coffee in ten centimetres of water as if it were the most natural thing in the world. Most of the streets have been raised in the past few years. You still have to paddle across Saint Mark's Square, albeit not for long. It is frequently flooded because it is only 90 centimetres above the average sea level. But the façade of the Basilica reflected in the shimmering water of Saint Mark's Square is an unforgettable sight.

Piacentini ▶I

Castello 4899, Ruga Giuffa, +39 041 5285971, closed Sunday and Monday (9 am–12.30 pm and 3 pm–7 pm)

Stefano repairs bags, shoes and zippers, but also does a nice line in handmade belts and leather or chamois leather garments. In fact, this is where bar owners come for their characteristic leather apron.

Tolin ▶F

Dorsoduro 3773, Ponte dei Vinanti, +39 041 5244090, closed Saturday afternoon, Sunday and Monday morning (8.30 am–1 pm and 3 pm–7.30 pm)

Footwear is Roberto Tolin's raison d'être. A wizard at bringing shoes, belts and leather goods back to life, he also makes shoes (€ 250-500) and boots to measure, including orthpaedic models.

masks and costumes

Traditionally, Venetian masks were made of leather or papier mâché. Their purpose was to conceal, and not to flaunt or astound. With the *tabarro*, the large black cloak, the three-pointed felt hat, and *baùta* or domino mask, the disturbing white papier mâché face made everyone – male and female – equal, ensuring the necessary anonymity for transgression. Today, shops full of gaudily coloured masks have taken over the city.

They are all the same, mere ceramic objects made who knows where that will eventually decorate the wall of some distracted tourist. Despite all this, there are still many craft mask makers who create, for sale or for hire, magnificent costumes such as dreams are made on.

Mondonovo ▶ M

Dorsoduro 3063, Rio Terà Canal, +39 041 5287344, closed Sunday (9 am–6.30 pm)

In his shop-cum-workshop, Guerrino Giano Lovato makes papier mâché masks of all shapes and sizes. The themes are myriad, and inspired by mythology or ancient legends.

One of Guerrino's most recent enterprises was recreating the sculptures and decorations for the auditorium of the La Fenice theatre.

Papier Maché ▶I

Castello 5175, Calle Lunga Santa Maria
Formosa, +39 041 5229995, open all week
(9 am–7.30 pm)

Stefano, Eliana and Manuela
make plates, statuettes and
wooden picture frames, but their main
line is papier mâché masks (€ 20-200), which
they paint meticulously in many different styles, from
oriental to Egyptian and De Stijl or Futurism-inspired.
This is one of the few shops that actually welcome very
young shoppers!

—57

Tragicomica ▶F

San Polo 2800, Calle dei Nomboli, +39 041 721102, open all week (10 am–7 pm)

Another great source of high-quality papier mâché masks,
ranging from the historic, like the *baùta* or the plague doctor,
to characters from the Commedia dell'Arte, mythology
or the mask maker's fertile imagination.
Costumes, complete with all the accoutrements,
can be hired here (€ 90-200 per day).

Ca' del Sol ▶I

Castello 4964, Fondamenta Osmarin, +39 041 5285549,
open all week (10 am–8 pm)

Amid and his helpers are all Iranian, but
for the past two decades they have been
making lace and leather masks in Venice.
Their signature products are decorated
papier mâché models (€ 20-200).
You can also buy a plain white mask at a very
reasonable price (€ 10-50) and paint it
yourself. Costume hire available.

58_

Ca' Macana ▶M

Dorsoduro 3172, Calle della Botteghe, +39 041 2776142,
open all week (10 am–6.30 pm)

Lots of masks, but this is also where
to come if you want to take a course
on the art of papier mâché.
When you walk past, you can often see
groups of intense-looking children gluing
or painting their latest creation.

Ca' Macana Atelier ▶A

Cannaregio 1374, Rio Terà San Leonardo,
+39 041 718655, open all week
(9 am–8 pm)

This is the lair of Carlos
Bassesco, the designer of
magnificent sets for cinema
and theatre. It is a treasure
trove of papier mâché masks
of all sizes and styles, including
Commedia dell'Arte, Carnival
and purely decorative.

Nicolao ▶H

Cannaregio 5565, Calle del Bagadin, +39 041 5207051, visits by appointment

Stefano Nicolao is much admired – and therefore impossibly busy – for his
unflagging commitment to technical, historical and philological research.
His costumes are sought after by theatres, opera companies,
film producers and the organisers of historic events.
You can hire one of them (€ 90-140 per day).

Le Burle Veneziane ▶N

San Marco 3436, Piscina San
Samuele, +39 041 5222150,
closed Sunday afternoon
(10.30 am–1 pm and 2 pm–7.30 pm)

A workshop with two souls. Grazia makes
costumes to measure (€ 1,200-9,000; for hire
at € 150-350 per day) with what can only be
described as obsessive attention to detail.
She creates 18th-century dames and dandies,
but also turns her hand to outfits
from the 1920s and kaftans.
Her partner Monica conjures up
superb copies of the jewellery of
the past, using only microscopic
beads. Admire the necklaces
(€ 55-150), rings (€ 25-60), earrings
and unusual forearm bracelets.

–59

Atelier Pietro Longhi ▶F

San Polo 2604b, Rio Terà dei Frari, +39 041 714478,
closed Saturday afternoon and Sunday
(10 am–12.30 pm and 3 pm–7 pm)

Behind their splendidly theatrical windows
looking onto the *rio terà* (infilled canal),
Francesco and Annamaria Briggi busily
put together costumes for the stage and
traditional festivals. If you want to hire
one for the day (€ 160-210), there are
plenty to choose from. Ancient Roman,
belle époque, Isabella d'Este and
Harlequin hang next to 18th-century
ceremonial dress and costumes
for the Doge's procession.
All the accessories are included:
wigs, costume jewellery, shoes,
weapons and shields.

glass pearls and beads

Glass beads, often called "pearls", have been made in Venice for many centuries. The local name, *conterie*, reminds us that they were used as currency in African markets, and as rosary beads. The art of making beads was inherited from the Romans. It earned Venice worldwide fame in the late 18th and early 19th centuries as the home of the glass beads (*margherite*) that emerged from the ovens of Murano, and of the handmade lampwork beads produced by countless small workshops all over the city. Today, we can admire the work of their successors. Glass beads of various sizes were strung together manually by women known as *impiraresse*, a name deriving from the verb *impirare*, to pierce, itself from the Greek *peiron*. Until not very long ago, you could see them sitting in the *calle* or the *campo* with their needles, threads and *sessola* (wooden workbox).

PERLINA FLOWERS

60_

The bunches of hand-strung beads were exported, to be used for decorating clothes or furnishings. Made by cutting up a glass rod, the beads can be small and round, or long (*pivette*), self-coloured or striped (*stricà*). Glass beads were used in Venice to make flowers, funeral wreaths, handbags, fringes, collars and a host of other objects.

FLORAL

Lampwork beads are made by fusing glass rods over the heat of a flame that once came from an oil lamp but today is fuelled by gas. The range of colours and shapes is vast.

ROSETTES

"PRIEST'S PEARLS"

The best-known articles in the Venetian tradition are the mosaic beads, made by inserting coloured murrines onto a monochrome base, *fiorato* or flowered beads, which have a strip of *avventurina* (glass with gold highlights) set in the midst of tiny roses, and gold or silver beads, which contain gold or silver leaf. Using special tweezers, the bead maker can coax the soft glass into a wide range of shapes.

One typically Venetian bead is the *rosetta*, said to have been invented in the 15th century by Maria Badover from Murano. They are made by cutting up a glass rod comprising various layers of colour (*sottane*), and grinding the pieces into shape.

Today, you can find genuine old Venetian beads from Africa and other markets, but only at considerable cost. Some glassmakers continue to produce beads to the ancient formula, using traditional techniques, and these are on sale at more affordable prices. In recent years, the markets of the west have been inundated by vast quantities of glass beads, large and small, from the far east or India, but the quality is inferior.

MICROMOSAICS

Zaggia ▶ N

Dorsoduro 1195, Calle de la Toletta, + 39 041 5223159, open Monday to Saturday, and often on Sunday (9 am–1 pm and 3.30 pm–7 pm)

A stone's throw from the Accademia is Nadia Viani's lovely store, full of wonderful small – and even smaller – things.
There are micromosaics and antique (€ 10-35) or old (€ 3-10) "pearls", which Nadia uses to make necklaces, bracelets and magnificent brooches at refreshingly affordable prices.

Anticlea ▶I

Castello 4719a, Calle San Provolo, +39 041 5286946, closed Sunday (10 am–7 pm)

Rita Turchetto sells Murano beads (€ 0.26-30), antique 19th-century beads and older ones, singly or in necklaces (€ 15-150). If you are sufficiently persuasive, she might show you one or two items from her personal collection.

Paropàmiso ▶H

San Marco 1701, Frezzeria, +39 041 5227120, closed Sunday winter only (10 am–7.30 pm)

The most respected bead shop in Venice and the one that has the finest collection of antique items, including glass *rosetta* (chevron) and Venetian beads, as well as others in agate, cornelian, coral, turquoise, lapis lazuli, amber, gold, wood, shell and various metals.

Many of the antique Venetian beads, some dating from the 17th century, come from Africa or the east, where Paropàmiso also sources jewellery, ethnic art and everyday objects.

Fabris ▶ ○

San Marco 2606, Campo San Maurizio, +39 041 5237054, closed Sunday (10 am–1 pm and 3.30 pm–7 pm)

Giulia is young, likeable and knows what's what. You can browse at leisure among the 1920s-style handbags in microscopic *conteria* beadwork, 18th-century centrepieces (€ 200-500), the odd engraving, period puppet theatres, micromosaics, bead flowers and leaves or antique fabrics.

_63

Costantini ▶ ○

San Marco 2668a, Campo San Maurizio, +39 041 739075, closed Sunday (10 am–1 pm and 4 pm–7 pm)

This shop sells mainly *conteria* beads by weight (€ 11 for old ones, € 6 for the slightly larger, brightly coloured new beads). You can also buy them in the form of necklaces, flowers, bows or evening bags.

Al Campanil ▶I

Castello 5184, Calle Lunga Santa
Maria Formosa, +39 041 5235734, closed
Sunday (9 am–12.30 pm and 3 pm–7.30 pm)

Sabina is a virtuoso decorator
on glass. She uses traditional
techniques and materials – oxides
and resins that she often goes to the
mountains to find – to make artistic
Murano glass and superb costume
jewellery, or produce glassware to
commission.

She also has lovely lampwork
bead necklaces she makes
herself (€ 25-200).

64_

Manù ▶O

San Marco 1228, Calle del Selvadego, +39 041 5229294,
closed Sunday (9.45 am–7.30 pm)

Just off the square in the narrowest
of *calli* is a shop where those in the know
can find beautifully made period Venetian
pearl, hard stone and other necklaces at
attractive prices.

La Perlina ▶F

San Polo 2559a, Fondamenta dei Frati, +39 041 714664, closed Sunday (10.30 am–6.30 am)

Fabio and Elisa opened this small, but very productive lampwork bead workshop
(€ 0.40-13). It's intriguing to see how these oddly named gems are made – *schissa*, *mina*,
varigola...

Perle e Dintorni ▶ H, G

San Marco 3740, Calle della Mandola, +39 041 5205068, closed
Sunday morning (9.30 am–1 pm and 2 pm–7.30 pm) San Marco 5468,
Sotoportego della Bissa, +39 041 5225624, closed Sunday morning (9.30
am–1 pm and 2 pm–7.30)

The shops are tad commercial, but they do offer a fun
range of imitation antique beads at attractive prices.
Buy them loose or made up into necklaces.

_65

Perle Veneziane ▶ I

Castello 4308, Ponte della Canonica, +39 041 5289059, open all week (10
am–1 pm and 6 pm–8 pm)

They've been making splendid lampwork beads
(€ 2-50) for three generations.
The coloured glass paste is worked, and
metal added to lend gold highlights to the
transparency of the glass.
The shop still offers necklaces
of microscopically small
19th-century beads.
These are the tiny "priest's
pearls", so small they look
almost like fabric, which
were used to adorn holy
vestments.

jewellery and bijouterie

Many jewellers offer brooches that feature a *moretto*, or blackamoor, as part of extensive ranges of antique jewels and modern equivalents made with traditional techniques. A classic, if not particularly politically correct motif, the *moretto* is portrayed with gold turban and waistcoat, enamel, pearls, hard stones in all colours, or even in diamonds and emeralds.

Vergombello ▶ O

San Marco 1565a, Ramo Secondo Corte Contarina, +39 041 5237821, closed Saturday afternoon and Sunday (9 am–7 pm)

Goldsmith to the city's wealthiest families, Vergombello is one of the most exclusive jewellery shops in Venice. Not content with this privileged status, Roberto continues to invent even more magnificent items. He creates brooches, rings and pendants with mechanisms – always jointed or screwed together, never glued – to conceal little secrets. Roberto's investment-casting equipment enables him to reproduce pieces to order.

Cipollato ▶ H

Castello 5336, Casselleria, +39 041 5228437, closed Monday (11 am–8 pm)

Sigfrido Cipollato is known above all for the *moretto* motifs that he makes into brooches and earrings. But he puts precisely the same skill and accuracy into all his other, one-off pieces of jewellery.

Laberintho ▶G

San Polo 2236, Calle del Scaleter, +39 041 710017,
closed Sunday and Monday (9.30 am–1 pm and 2.30 pm–7 pm)

Maddalena, Marco and Davide create
wonderful earrings and rings (€ 700-1,000)
with inlaid hard stones, such as lapis lazuli,
turquoise, coral and opal. But their strong
suit is necklaces (€ 1,000-1,700) made
from tiny sheets of ground glass that are
fashioned using a very complex technique.
They are reminiscent of light reflecting on
the seabed.

Mejorin ▶I

Castello 4504, Campo San Zaccaria, +39 041 7241033,
closed Sunday (9 am–12 pm and 4 pm–7 pm)

Piero could be considered a sculptor,
an inventor or an experimenter.
What is certain is that he is an eclectic,
reserved individual of the type it is getting
hard to find in an increasingly glossy city.
He makes jewellery and other objets d'art
in precious and non-precious metals.

ABC ▶ G

Santa Croce 1839, Calle del Tentor, +39 041 5244001, closed Sunday and Monday
(9.30 am–12.30 pm and 3.30 pm–7.30 pm)

Andrea d'Agostino experiments with ancient techniques, combining archaeology with his other professional skills. He uses the Etruscan-Phoenician method of granulation, decorating objects with grains of gold that are not welded, but instead held fast by colloidal reaction. Other techniques like damask or mokume gane enable him to combine different alloys to create exciting effects of colour, movement and light.

Attombri ▶ H

San Polo 74, Sotoportego degli Oresi, +39 041 5212524,
closed Sunday (9.30 am–1 pm and 2.30 pm–7 pm)

Stefano and Daniele make necklaces
(from € 60), earrings (€ 45-75), cufflinks,
bracelets, brooches and household
ornaments with antiallergic alloy or silver
wire, assembled with antique Venetian
beads. Their output is much in favour with
young people of the New Age persuasion,
the minimal-chic crowd and women who just
like to make an impression.

Gualti ▶ M

Dorsoduro 3111, Rio Terà Canal,
+39 041 5201731, closed Sunday
(10 am–1 pm and 3 pm–7.30 pm)

Gualtiero's petite but high-
spirited accessories have always
been beloved of Venice's elegant
women, who save them for special occasions. He offers
earrings, brooches (from € 60), necklaces, bracelets
and even glass-like hat pieces. The synthetic resins are
shaped into organic designs that are soft to the touch
and apparently fragile, with glass balls trapped inside. He
also makes shoes (€ 219) with an 8.5-cm heel, or 5 cm for the less
audacious, complete with matching pochettes in 85 shades of silk satin.

_69

Fescina ▶ H

San Marco 4458, Calle dei Fuseri, +39 041 5207882,
closed Saturday and Sunday (9.30 am–2 pm)

In her small workshop, goldsmith Stefania Fescina calmly assembles
antique buttons, coins, oriental glass beads and stones with metal
and wire to make stunning brooches, necklaces and bracelets
(€ 150-750). If the shop is closed when you drop by, do come back.
Artists can be unpredictable!

lacework and embroidery

Burano lace is made using only needle and
thread, with no fabric support, hence its name
punto in aria, literally "air stitch".
The technique starts with the main outline,
the so-called "warp", which goes all round the
pattern prepared on coloured paper.
Using the warp as a base, the light and shade of
the pattern is filled in with Venetian stitch, which
has a bar background, or Burano stitch, with a net
background, to mention the two most widely used.

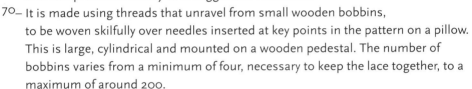

Bobbin, or pillow, lace was second in importance only to Burano lace,
and was produced chiefly at Chioggia and Palestrina.

70– It is made using threads that unravel from small wooden bobbins,
to be woven skilfully over needles inserted at key points in the pattern on a pillow.
This is large, cylindrical and mounted on a wooden pedestal. The number of
bobbins varies from a minimum of four, necessary to keep the lace together, to a
maximum of around 200.
In the past, as many as 1,500 bobbins have been used.
For any given thickness of thread, the lace produced is less taut than needlelace.
For centuries, lace was an important economic resource for Burano, but changes
in taste and women's liberation first, then mechanised lacemaking and imports
of low-cost products from the Far East, are all contributing to the final demise
of this ancient tradition.

The last attempts to save the
industry failed when the lace
school and consortium closed.
Today, only the museum at
Burano remains, along with one
or two teachers who make
a few items to sell privately.

Largo Micheli ▶ H

San Marco 318, Calle Canonica,
+39 041 5229581,
open all week (9 am–7 pm)

This large store very close to Piazza San Marco has a fine range of household linen and tablecloths, embroidered by hand and decorated with lace of all types. Prices are affordable. You can also admire the genuine Burano and pillow lace displayed on the walls.

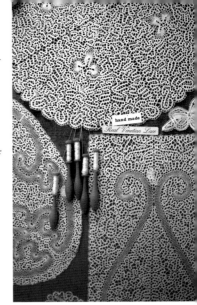

Jesurum ▶ H

San Marco 4857, Mercerie del Capitello,
+39 041 5206177, open all week
(10 am–7.30 pm, Sunday 10.30 am–6.30 pm)

A great place to buy table, bed and bathroom linen, as well as lace. The Jesurum collection offers reliably good-quality reinterpretations of the Venetian lace and embroidery heritage, although nowadays some of the work is mechanised. You'll find classic and romantic articles embellished with lace and entre-deux embroidery in whites, ecrus, blues, greens and golden yellows.

Annelie ▶ M

Dorsoduro 2748, Calle Lunga San Barnaba, +39 041 5203277,
closed Saturday afternoon and Sunday (9.30 am–12.30 pm and 4 pm–7.30 pm)

A cornucopia of white linen and cotton in a cosy profusion of lingerie bags, nightshirts, pillowslips and sheets. Made-to-measure items include baby and newborn clothes, as well as tablecloths and curtains. They'll also embroider initials on towels and household linen for you.

 # fabrics

If you have ever fallen in love with the sumptuous clothes and drapes in the paintings of Paolo Veronese – in the 16th-century, the city boasted 5,000 working looms – come to Venice. Brocades, damasks, lampas, *soprarizzo* (cut and uncut) velvet, satin and velvets are still produced to ancient cartoons and original designs.

Spanish-born

Mariano Fortuny y Madrazo (1871–1949)
was a great innovator in a number of fields. A painter, set designer and photographer, he also invented marvellous furnishing fabrics, inspired by Venetian and Florentine brocades and *inferriato* (voided) velvets from the late 15th and 16th centuries. Whether his fabrics are simple cottons, or silk or cotton velvets, they are all printed using techniques so special that they look almost hand-painted. Fortuny loved to mix periods, fusing the Renaissance with the 17th century, and geographical origins, sometimes juxtaposing oriental motifs with ancient African tribal symbols. His clothes were inspired by ancient Greece and Venetian paintings, which he drew on for the patterns of his fabrics, his theatrical costumes and his fashionwear.
All the most celebrated figures of the day wore Fortuny clothes on stage and in real life, including Isadora Duncan, Eleonora Duse, Sarah Bernardt, Peggy Guggenheim and Emma and Irma Gramatica. Fortuny reinterpreted the kimono, the burnouse, the djellaba, the sari and the dolman, occasionally embellishing them with delicately coloured Murano *perline*. His Delphos tunic was a classic. A tube-like, figure-flattering satin, taffeta and silk gauze dress, it was very finely pleated and tied with a cord at the waist. Fortuny lived and worked in Venice in a palazzo in Campo San Beneto, which was gifted to the local authority in 1956. Today, it is called Palazzo Fortuny, and is used a museum. Palazzo Fortuny is one of the few 20th-century environmental museums. Visitors can inspect Fortuny's workshop.
The remaining spaces provide a venue for exhibitions and other arts-related activities. There are printed cloths, fabrics, clothing, period costumes, paintings and weapons, as well as a major photographic archive containing more than 12,000 glass negatives and 2,000 photographic prints.

Tessuti Artistici Fortuny ▶ s

mill Giudecca 805, Fondamenta San Biagio, +39 041 5224078,
closed Saturday and Sunday (9 am–12.30 pm and 2 pm–5 pm)

The mill continues to make the products created
by Fortuny in the 1920s. These are remarkable not just
for their patterns but also for the way the cotton is treated and the printing process,
which are very much top secret.

The results are stunning. The fabrics feel almost like silk, and the colours take on a thousand nuances
and contrasts, setting gold off with green, green with ochre or red with yellow. Each bolt is unique.

Trois ▶ o

San Marco 2666, Campo San Maurizio,
+39 041 5222905, closed Sunday and
Monday morning (10 am–1 pm and 4
pm–7.30 pm)

Noted for its range of Fortuny
fabrics, of which it still has a
good stock, Trois also offers
18th-century Venetian antique
items and other intriguing
furnishing accessories.

Bevilacqua ▶ A, I, O

mill and showroom Santa Croce 1320, Campiello de la Comare, +39 041 721566, closed Sunday (9 am–5.30 pm, visits by appointment)
shop San Marco 337b, Ponte della Canonica, +39 041 5287581, open all week (10 am–7 pm; Sunday until 5 pm);
shop San Marco 2520, Campo Santa Margherita del Giglio, +39 041 2410662, open all week (9.30 am–1.30 pm and 3.30 pm–7 pm)

74_ Bevilacqua has been making and selling Venetian velvets, damasks and brocades since 1875.

The furnishing fabrics are so lavishly worked that you feel you ought to use them for clothes. If you ever have to furnish the *piano nobile* (main floor) of a palazzo on the Canal Grande, this is where to come for the appropriate velvets, tapestries and cushions. Most of the fabrics are still produced at the Venice mill using 18th-century wooden looms and exclusive patterns. The Bevilacqua archive contains more than 3,500 models.

Rubelli ▶G

San Marco 3877, Palazzo Corner Spinelli, +39 041 5236110,
closed Saturday and Sunday (8.30 am–12.30 pm and 3.30 pm–7.30 pm)

Although it has now turned into a multinational
that manufactures in Como and Pennsylvania,
the heart of this historic weaving mill, founded in 1858 by
Lorenzo Rubelli, has stayed here in Venice.
In the showroom on the Canal Grande, you can
choose from brocades, damasks, velvets, silks and
lampas fabrics that grace museums, castles and royal
residences.
Most of the raw materials are natural fibres, including
silk, linen, cotton and wool, with added first-quality
viscose that gives the fabrics the feel of silk.
There is also a range of fireproof fabrics.
The collection ranges from the simplest of cottons
(€ 60) to sumptuous damasks in organzine silk (€ 390).

Helene ▶N

Dorsoduro 683, Calle della Chiesa,
+39 041 5237605, closed Sunday and Tuesday
(4 am–7 pm)

Hélène Kuhn dyes, prints
and paints silks with modern
decorations and motifs.
She contrives to obtain magical
multicoloured transparent silks,
nocturnal or metallic highlights on
velvet and rich, graphic colours on cotton.
Each piece is unique and if you like, you can have your favourite made
into an exclusive jacket (€ 400-600), scarf (€ 120) or wall hanging (€ 400-1,500).

Venetia Studium ▶○

San Marco 2403, Calle Larga XXII Marzo, +39 041 5229281, open all week (9 am–7.30 pm)

This is one of those shops where you can find clothing, lamps (from € 240),
evening bags, shawls, cushions, bows and other furnishing accessories inspired
by Mariano Fortuny's pleated technique. The scarves (€ 50-200) in 70 or so different
shades make an attractive informal gift.

Cattana ▶N

San Marco 3357, Calle Mocenigo, +39 041 5224369,
closed Sunday and Monday morning (10 am–1 pm
and 4 pm–7 pm)

Chiarastella Cattana is an expert consultant interior designer.
Here at her base close to Palazzo Grassi we can admire the
elegant simplicity of her selections, such as designer wrought-iron tables and glass sculptures by
Ritsue Mishima. Chiarastella personally supervises the manufacture and patterns of her specially
commissioned cotton and linen soft furnishings (€ 100-160, height 3 metres).

Il Canapè ▶F

Dorsoduro 3736, San Pantalon, +39 041 714264,
closed Sunday and Monday morning (9 am–12.45 pm
and 3.15 pm–7.30 pm; closed Saturday afternoon in summer)

A great place to come if you're thinking about making
over your home. There's a good choice of mainly
French and Italian trims and textiles for curtains, sofas,
armchairs, chairs and beds, as well as one or two
selected accessories. But the big attraction here is the
meticulous bespoke upholstery service.

Arras ▶N

Dorsoduro 3235, Campiello dei Squelini, +39 041 5226460, closed Sunday
(9 am–1 pm and 3.30 pm–7.30 pm)

The workshop is run by a co-operative for
the recovery of differently able youngsters.
They loom weave colourful fabrics with a
slightly grungy look from silk, linen, wool
and cotton, then make them into jackets
(from € 200), shawls (from € 50) and
scarves (from € 28). Fabrics, blankets,
bedspreads, hangings and carpets can
be made to order.

carpets

Don't be surprised at the large numbers of carpets depicted in Italian and European paintings. In the 14th and 15th centuries, Italy and Venice in particular were the world's leading importers of oriental carpets. Magnificent examples arrived in the lagoon from the east, to be sold all over Italy.

Rillosi ► N

Dorsoduro 3280, Calle del Capeler, +39 041 5205887, closed Sunday and Monday (10 am–12 pm and 3.30 pm–7 pm)

Augusto Rillosi has an inquisitive mind. A bibliophile, he studies a thousand different subjects, including ancient fabrics. You feel you are in good hands with Augusto. He can offer kilim rugs and Tibetan, Chinese, Turkish or Iranian fabrics from the 17th century to the early 19th, not to mention interesting oriental objets d'art.

FRAGMENT OF LATE 17TH-CENTURY CHINESE NINGXIA CARPET

The kilims that Augusto has woven for him in Turkey – he supervises the weavers personally – are stunning with their graphic, unfussy patterns. The quality of his products is further enhanced by the handspun woollen yarn and exclusively natural dyes used, including madder (purple red), cochineal (scarlet), chamomile, indigo and walnut husk.

78_

Rashid Rahaim & C. ►○

San Marco 2380, Calle Large XXII Marzo, +39 041 5224736, closed Sunday (9 am–12.30 pm and 3 pm–7.30 pm)

Franco dell'Orto has a vast assortment of old carpets, most notably the very large decorative carpets and rugs from the Caucasus that are his specialty. But he also offers Persian carpets, and 16th or 17th-century tapestries from Europe. Franco's stock includes a fine array of European carpets, especially Spanish-woven decorative floor coverings.

Saraji Gallery ►F

Santa Croce 971, Calle Larga dei Bari, +39 041 714894, closed Sunday and Monday morning (9.30 am–12.30 pm and 4 pm–7.15 pm)

Saraji Gallery imports modern carpets from Iran and the orient at affordable prices. Carpet washing (€ 20 per square metre) and restoration services are also available. If you walk past, you may well find Abbas Thran working away, oblivious to the world.

antiques and modern collectables

The golden years of antique shopping in Venice may be past, but there are still places where you can find unusual, exciting pieces that do not have to shatter your spending plans. Naturally, you need a sharp eye and lots of patience. There are serious antique dealers who won't touch anything that isn't at least a couple of hundred years old, as well as secondhand shops where a 1970s lighter might be considered collectable.

Codognato ▶○

San Marco 1295, Calle Seconda dell'Ascensione, +39 041 5225042, closed Sunday and Monday morning (10 am–1 pm and 4 pm–7 pm)

This is where to come for special items at stunningly expensive prices. You'll see antique, modern and Art Deco jewellery, laps lazuli-decorated silver plates, keepsakes, antique cameos, alabaster, serpentine, amethyst, rock crystal, agate and chalcedony engraved using techniques 2,000 years old.

Attilio Codognato is widely respected as a collector and expert on contemporary art.

Bastianello ▶H

San Marco 5042, Campo San Bartolomeo, +39 041 5226751,
open all week (10.30 am–7.30 pm)

A superb treasure trove of a workshop where Giovanni Bastianello is now helped by his children, Emanuela and Gianluca, as he designs and makes his own line of jewellery. Around them is a rich collection of household articles and antique jewels dating from the 18th century onwards. Choose from the 18th-century ivory and silverware, glass-paste Art Deco dome lamps, Viennese porcelain tea sets, or English, German and French silver. The owners' predilection for long case and table clocks is obvious.

Scarpa ▶ N

Dorsoduro 1023, Accademia, +39
041 5239700, closed Sunday (9.30
am–12.45 pm and 3.30 pm–7 pm)

As you come out of the
Gallerie dell'Accademia,
you find a small *calle*
where a shop with large
windows flaunts superb
large-scale canvases. If
you have the wherewithal,
this is where you can
by a Tiepolo, a Longhi
or a Guardi. For you
have discovered the
fabulous display area of
the antiquarian and bibliophile, Pietro Scarpa, whose services are often called upon by scholars and
museum curators all over the world. Paintings, sculpture, graphic art, drawings, archaeological remains
and contemporary items are all there awaiting your scrutiny.

Zanutto ▶ N

San Marco 3462, Calle delle Botteghe, +39 041 5235359,
closed Sunday (10 am–12.30 pm and 4 pm–7.30 pm)

Vincenzo Zanutto offers mainly Venetian
paintings, as well as some antique Italian
or Dutch works, still lifes, landscapes and
portraits from the 16th and 17th centuries.
He and his daughter Elisabetta are also
much in demand as restorers of paintings.

Mirate ▶ ○

San Marco 1904, Calle della Verona, +39 041 5227600,
closed Sunday and Monday morning
(10 am–12 pm and 4 pm–7 pm)

Francesco Saverio Mirate's antique shop
has paintings and furniture dating from
the 14th to the 19th century.
Francesco has no particular specialisation.
He knows it all!

Antichità San Samuele ▶ N

San Marco 3130, Calle delle Botteghe, +39 041 5204900,
closed Sunday and Monday (11 am–1 pm and 5 pm–7.30 pm)

Silvana Vianello's main interests are in the field of medieval and
Renaissance sculpture, but she lavishes the same meticulous care
on the many other items she sells to grace formal residences.

L'Angelo Narciso ▶ N

San Marco 3135, Piscina San Samuele, +39 041 5202450, closed Sunday
(10 am–1 pm and 4 pm–7.30 pm)

In this small shop, Valentina Chiais has a range of Baroque-period
articles, especially her favourites, angels. She can offer you carved
ones, gilt ones, angel brackets, angels bearing candelabra, putto
angels and cherubs.

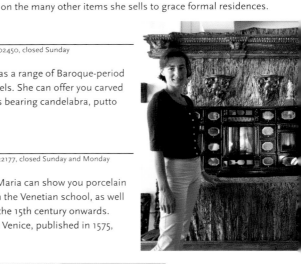

Kleine Galerie ▶ N

San Marco 2972, Calle delle Botteghe, +39 041 5222177, closed Sunday and Monday
morning (10 am–12.30 pm and 4 pm–7.30 pm)

Claudio Gorini and his son Federico Maria can show you porcelain
and a few 18th-century paintings from the Venetian school, as well
as rare books, maps and prints from the 15th century onwards.
How much do you think that guide to Venice, published in 1575,
might cost?

Antiquus ▶ N

San Marco 3131, Calle delle Botteghe,
+39 041 5206395, closed Sunday
and Monday morning (10 am–12.30 pm
and 3 pm–7.30 pm)

Oreste Caniato has eminently
collectable silverware, a few
paintings by 18th and
19th-century masters,
and furniture and other items
in the Empire, Directory and
Biedermeier styles.

Arga ▶ G

San Marco 3659, Rio Terà dei Assassini, +39 041 2411124,
closed Sunday and Monday (10.30 am–1 pm and 3.30 pm–7 pm)

Gabriella Tallon is a connoisseur of eastern art
who is much esteemed, even by her hard-to-please
peers. The elegant gallery sets out antique canvases,
statues and vases from Tibet, Gandhara,
India and China.

_83

Totem Gallery ▶ N

Dorsoduro 878b, Accademia, +39 041 5223641,
closed Sunday (10 am–1 pm and 3 pm–7 pm)

Claudio Gatta and Johannes Hendrik Du Toit
can show you terra cotta, bronze, brass, iron,
bone and ivory articles of African tribal art from the
19th century – or even earlier – that they have picked
up on their extensive travels.
The gallery of contemporary art next door has an
exhibition of works by interesting emerging artists.

Antichità Marciana ▶○

San Marco 1691, Frezzaria, +39 041 5235666, closed Sunday and Monday morning (9.30 am–1 pm and 3.30 pm–7.30 pm)

The show room is fantastic, and if you ask there are also other rooms to visit. You can savour the atmosphere of 18th-century Venice among the furniture, paintings and collector's items from the orient. Visitors will note the Mirella Spinella fabrics – dyed and hand-printed silk velvet with exclusive patterns – that can be purchased by the metre (€ 150), or made into cushions, jackets, bags and superb tapestry bedspreads.

Ferruzzi ▶○

Dorsoduro 368, Fondamenta Ospedaletto, +39 041 5205996, closed Tuesday afternoon (10 am–1 pm and 2.30 pm–6.30 pm)

Robi comes from a family of artists who have instilled in him a passion for pottery and majolica. If you can find him, and you know your ceramics, a visit could be the opportunity for an enthralling discussion.

Markets are organised frequently throughout the year. Bargains are there to be snapped up by shoppers who know what they are looking for:

• *Campo San Maurizio* antiques market (information from Associazione Espositori di Campo San Maurizio, +39 328 0334032)

• *Campo Santa Maria Nova* – Miracoli, flea market and secondhand market (information: Consiglio di Quartiere 1, +39 041 2710022, +39 041 2710015)

• *Via Garibaldi*, experimental antiques and collectables market (information: public space trading office, +39 041 2747236)

Il Mercante del Cammello ▶ B

Palazzo Correr, Cannaregio 2217, +39 041 721811, closed Saturday and Sunday
(8.30 am–12.30 pm and 2.30 pm–6.30 pm)

Well off the beaten track, Adriana Maschietto has plenty
of space for the wealth of objects large and small she can
show you. You might find a 19th-century piano, a Murano
chandelier, an Art Deco headboard, a romantic antique
sideboard, a precious late 19th-century conteria beadwork
funeral wreath, German-made scales from the 1940s,
new 1930s-1980s clothes, Indian batiks or Chinese silks.

Finarte Semenzato ▶ B

Palazzo Correr, Cannaregio 2217, +39 041 721811, closed Saturday
and Sunday (8.30 am–12.30 pm and 2.30 pm–6.30 pm)

This famous auction house has monopolised
the Venetian antique market since the 1960s.
Themed auctions are organised once a month,
usually on Saturday and Sunday. Antique furnishings,
Italian and European furniture, collectables, objets
d'art, paintings, period jewellery, silver, bronze, ivory, engravings, drawings, watercolours, carpets,
books and sculpture. Occasionally, the furnishings and contents of entire villas or galleries go
under the hammer. This melting pot of a market attracts a heterogeneous clientele.

Art Studio ▶ O

San Marco 3821, Ponte dei Frati, +39 347 9801466, closed Sunday (10 am–7 am)

When you emerge in Campo Sant'Angelo, and before you go over the bridge, you will

see on your left
some curious
objects peeking
out of a door.
If you are invited in,
you will find a large space
where you can browse through
the objects that Rossella
Costantini digs out on her
peregrinations. The emphasis
is on bijouterie and antiques.

Quel Che Manca ▶ G

San Marco 3965, Campo San Beneto, +39 041 5222681, closed Sunday (summer only) and Monday (11 am–7pm)

A small *calle* near the very central Calle della Mandorla is where you will find a shop that many local interior designers know and love.

There is more space than you generally find in Venetian stores so the chances of coming across *quel che manca* (what's missing) are high! Furniture and collectables are sold directly or on commission.

Gervasutti ▶ L

Castello 3725, Campo Bandiera e Moro or della Bragora, +39 041 5236777, +39 348 4022950, closed Sunday (10 am–3 pm), visits by appointment

A friendly shop on Campo Bandiera e Moro, in one of the least visited parts of the city. In this pleasant neighbourhood, Venice feels like a small, quiet town. You're more likely to find Sara in the shop while her brother Michele is out looking for antique furniture, chairs and armchairs. But Michele also picks up theatre sets and costumes, mosaic mirrors and modern collectables.

Ballarin ▶ı

Castello 4557, Salizada del Pistor, +39 347 9635115, closed Sunday (4 pm–8 pm)

Valter is an old-fashioned secondhand dealer at heart. He tracks down and offers for sale almost anything, from period furniture to modern ashtrays, 19th-century leaf chandeliers and 1960s designer lamps. Antiquarians, bibliophiles and experts of all kinds come here to browse and rummage. And if you have a sharp eye, you can pick up some great bargains!

Al Mercatippy ▶c

Cannaregio 4557, Salizada del Pistor, +39 347 9635115, closed Sunday (4 pm–8 pm)

Maurizio Bolla is leading figure at Venice's secondhand markets. His little shop has small – and very small – modern collectables galore. Admire his keyrings, watches, alarm clocks, collectable tins, vases and mysterious, unidentifiable ornaments.

Canestrelli ▶o

Dorsoduro 364a, Campiello Barbaro, +39 041 5227072, closed Sunday (10.30 am–1 pm and 3 pm–5.30 pm)

Claudia's delightful little shop is where to come for antiques, cupboards, votive objects, bronze doors, wooden angels, bronzes, engravings, antique costume jewellery and the thousand other objects she finds on her expeditions.

restoration and gilding

As well as antique and art shops, Venice also has workshops where furniture and other objects are made or restored, in a vaguely oriental and very atmospheric hotchpotch. There have always been many different kinds of woodworker in the city, from the *marangòn da grosso* (carpenter) and *marangòn da sutìlo* (cabinetmaker) to *indoradòr* (gilder) and *depentòr*, master of the ancient technique of lacquering furniture, picture frames and console tables with floral motifs, landscapes, country scenes or chinoiserie.

Miani ▶F

San Polo 2898b, Calle del Campaniel,
+39 041 5211312, closed Saturday
afternoon and Sunday (9 am–12 pm
and 3 pm–6.30 pm)

In this workshop, you can breathe in the atmosphere of a *lacadòr* (lacquerer) and *indoradòr* (gilder) among angels, *moretti* (blackamoors) and superbly decorated headboards.

The archangel Gabriel who looks down on you from the bell tower of Saint Mark's was gilded ten or so years ago by Adriano Miani.

Cavalier ▶N

San Marco 2863a, Campo Santo
Stefano, +39 041 5238621, closed
Sunday (10 am–7 pm)

Alberto Cavalier has now
taken over from his father
in this characteristic
gilding, lacquering and
restoration workshop
looking onto Campo Santo
Stefano. He also makes
period articles and works
to drawings. Among his
gilt frames and masks,
you can find traditional
moretto doorstops and
hand-carved wooden
lampstands decorated
in gold or silver leaf.
They portray young
black servants, as was
fashionable at the height
of the Most Serene
Republic's wealth
and splendour.

_89

90— **Cicogna** ► F

San Polo 2867, Campo San Tomà, +39 041 5227678, closed Saturday afternoon and Sunday
(8.30 am–12.30 pm and 3.30 pm–7.30 pm; also closed Saturday morning in summer)

The beautifully arranged windows on the *campo* display gilt
chairs upholstered in turquoise velvet, and chests painted in
fresh, clear 18th century-style colours. Michele Cicogna also
makes ornaments, frames and furniture enhanced by traditional
lacquering and gilding. His copies on panel or canvas of old
Venetian paintings are simply wonderful.

Bedon ► H

Cannaregio 4467, Campiello drio la Chiesa, Santi Apostoli, +39 339 4847799,
closed Sunday (9.30 pm–7 pm)

After taking a degree in architecture and practising for a few
years, Isabella yielded to her passion for gilding, lacquering
and restoring fine furniture.

Buggio ▶F

San Polo 2423, Calle de l'Ogio e del Caffettier, +39 041 719890, often open on
Sunday and sometimes closed on other days (10 am–1 pm and 4 pm–8 pm)

Before you visit this workshop, which looks more like a hobbyist's
garage, you might want to brush up on the corpuscular theory
of light. Luciano Buggio, who has a degree in sociology, is an
enthusiastic student of physics and related areas. Here in his lair,
he transforms pieces of furniture by mixing components and styles
with effortless skill. Two bedside cabinets could become a dresser,
a chest of drawers might morph into a writing desk, and bottles
are frequently startled to find they have turned into vases.
Luciano is an expert re-user. Unlike recyclers, who turn everything
into pulp, he strives to respect the work that has gone into each
of the pieces he manipulates. He is well worth getting to know.

Artù ▶I

Castello 6656, Barbaria de le Tole, +39 041 2777838, +39 349 5273473,
closed Sunday (10 am–1 pm and 3 pm–7 pm)

Antonio Casellati and Tobia Morra are problem solvers.
This is where discriminating Venetians come to have their
antique furniture restored. Antonio and Tobia also use
traditional techniques for decorations, as well as recovering
or recreating articles in wood or stone.

Mason ▶M

Dorsoduro 1606b, Calle dei Preti, +39 320 0615881, visits by appointment

Elisabetta Mason continues the family business
in the spacious workshop where she restores,
gilds and decorates picture frames and antiques.

furnishing accessories

In its long history, Venice has been something of a magpie, picking up bright shiny objects all over the world and bringing them back to her nest. If you want to create a Venetian atmosphere in your own home, browse through tapestries, Persian, Caucasian and Chinese carpets, bronzes, jades, mosque lamps, damask fabrics, lace, gilt candelabra, blackamoor lampholders, leaded glass doors and partitions, sumptuous drapery, ivory, crystal, painted chinoiserie, miniatures, Chinese porcelain, Rococo glass cups and gilt or lacquered console tables, trays and picture frames.

What are a Chinese jade Buddha and an 18th-century glass barley sugar-twist mirror doing among Japanese masks, Indian fabrics, Persian carpets, Turkish bric-a-brac, damask curtains and a papier mâché column? Try going into a traditional Venetian reception room, or one of the many expensive markets scattered around the city, and you'll see they go perfectly well together. The art of combinations – harmoniously bringing together objects of different materials, styles, periods and purposes – is one of the most highly prized skills on the Venetian social scene.

Trevisanello ▶ N

Dorsoduro 662, Campo San Vio, +39 041 5207779, closed Sunday (9.30 am–1 pm and 4 pm–7.45 pm)

This craft workshop produces picture frames. Pietro is carrying on a family tradition, making his classic frames for museums and galleries, while his sister, Silvia, creates photograph frames and small mirrors decorated with glass pearls, leaves and flowers. The results are attractive, and needn't be expensive.

Canestrelli ▶N

Dorsoduro 1173, Calle de la Toletta, +39 041 2770617, closed Sunday (10.30 am–1 pm and 3.30 pm–7 pm)

The most famous *Oeil de Sorcière* (literally, "witch's eye") is the one in the background of Van Eyck's *Arnolfini Portrait*.

The magical convex mirror, known since ancient times for its ability to reflect a wide angle of vision, is Stefano Coluccio's passion. He creates endless variations on the theme, always taking his inspiration from drawing or paintings. What's more, his pieces are even said to bring good luck.

A Mano ▶F

San Polo 2616, Rio Terà, +39 041 715742, closed Sunday (10 am–1.30 pm and 2.30 pm–7.30 pm)

Alessandro Salvadori is always busy dreaming up marvellous light fittings for extravagant homes. He has moving lamps (€ 135-300), mobiles, lampshades, frames (€ 40-200), mirrors and a vast array of ornaments in copper, iron, brass, bamboo, gauze, glass and fabric.

Il Milione ▶ H

Castello 6025, Campo Santa Marina, +39 041 2410722,
closed Sunday (10 am–12.30 pm and 3 pm–7 pm)

In his small workshop, Daniele Zampedri
makes beautiful hand-painted silk lampshades,
decorated in Fortuny style with glass pearls.
Prices are reasonable (€ 200-300).

Cenerentola ▶ F

San Polo 2718, Calle dei Saoneri, +39 041 5232006,
closed Sunday (10.30 am–1 pm and 2.30 pm–8 pm)

Lidia Vallongo makes 18th century-style lampshades
with anything that takes her fancy. She might use
embroidered pillowcases, camisoles,
lace or ecclesiastical fabrics.
She can make items to order
in just a few days. Lidia quite
justifiably boasts that she
brings old things back to
useful life. One customer
even has what was once
a countess's underwear
gracing her front room.

Greco ▶ O

San Marco 2433, Ponte de le Ostreghe, +39 041 5234573,
open all week (9.30 am–1 pm and 3 pm–7.30 pm)

Sisters Rita and Rosy, ever at work on some new creation, greet you
with open arms in this city-centre workshop from another age. They
are known and respected by the great and the good of Venice for
their lampshades, and their clientele includes many visitors from
the United States. That probably explains why the sisters are so
familiar with North American electrical standards.

Rossi ▶B

Cannaregio 2543, Fondamenta della Misericordia, +39 041 717735,
open all week (5 pm–8.30 pm, Saturday and Sunday 3 pm–8.30 pm)

Luigino's electrical and plumbing goods store catches your eye
with its amazing collection of taps, keys and household devices
of all kinds. The owner is one of those rare individuals who knows
how to take things apart and put them together again.
If you have a broken lamp, tap or whatever, Luigino will fix it.
He is especially in demand when old aristocratic homes are being
restored. If a light fitting needs to be taken apart, Luigino will be
there individually dismantling each glass pearl or metal fixing.

Trame di Luce ▶M

Dorsoduro 2834a, Ponte dei
Pugni, +39 041 5226821, closed
Saturday and Sunday (5 pm–8 pm)

Marcello Moretti only opens in the evenings.
He started what is fast becoming his main business
activity by fixing his friends' irons, toasters and mixers.
Everyone needs a friend like Marcello.
In his pocket-sized workshop, he transforms candelabra
and table legs, assembles light fittings, repairs lamps
and creates curious sconces and lampshades (€ 15-200),
to match with a base in wood, glass or brass.

—95

Franzato ▶G

Santa Croce 2155a, Calle Longa, +39 041 5240770,
open all week (10 am–1 pm and 3 pm–7 pm)

Marco Franzato makes artistic
windows with lead binding
(from € 250 per square metre),
to order if necessary, household
ornaments and necklaces using the
Tiffany copper foil binding technique.
He is happy to discuss the design of
his attractive multicoloured objects
with prospective clients.

 # wood

In order to emerge as a city of stone, Venice has had to acquire a soul of wood. The millions of poles that support the city in the lagoon mud, the ceiling beams, the stairs to top floors and the light, flexible inside walls in the houses have consumed vast quantities of timber over the centuries.

The long, complicated woodworking production chain included foresters, bargees, workers in the Arsenale, carpenters, *marangòni da casa* (builders), ceiling and wooden wall workers, *marangòni da noghera* (cabinetmakers) and furniture makers. Some specialist trades survive. There are *squeraròli* (gondola builders), the odd *remèr* (oarmaker), restorers, furniture and gondola upholsterers, door and gate makers, *marangòni da soàze* (frame makers), *indoradòri* (gilders) and *lacadòri* (lacquerers), wood carvers, one or two makers of musical instruments, antiquarians and secondhand dealers. For *marangòni da noghèra*, *marangòni da soàze*, and makers of shelves, festoons, door decorations, angel, cherub and blackamoor candleholders, friezes and wall lights, wood is not simply something to carve. It is a material to etch, shape, bloat, distend and smooth, removing sharp edges and precise geometrical shapes. Wood is camouflaged and brought to life with veneers, shelves, arches, columns, bows, rosettes, gilding, coloured or translucent lacquers, chinoiserie, faint figures or idyllic landscapes in pale pastel shades. All this requires manual and technical ability, the selection of the right timber, hundreds of cutting and carving implements, as well as a knowledge of materials, dies and formulae to prepare special glues and paints made by mixing natural earths, ground minerals and pigments.

The **fòrcola** (rowlock) and oar are the engine of a Venetian boat. They are constructed by specialist craft workers.
Fòrcole have complex shapes and come in all sizes from 45 to 100 centimetres, depending on the kind of boat on which they will be mounted, the gondola *fòrcola* being the most elaborate.
It is generally made of walnut or cherry wood, but maple or pear may also be used. Oars, too, are constructed using special techniques that vary from vessel to vessel.

Pastor – Le Fòrcole ▶ O

Dorsoduro 341, Fondamenta Soranzo
de la Fornace, +39 041 5225699, closed
Sunday (8 am–12 pm and 1 pm–6 pm)

Saverio is the dean of
oarmakers. He collaborates
with champion gondoliers in
his constant efforts to improve
the performance and aesthetic
appeal of his *fòrcole* (rowlocks).
Saverio is willing to try new
materials, while remaining
faithful to the techniques and
tools of the Venetian tradition.
He is also the founder and
chair of the *El Fèlze* association
for craft workers involved in
gondola making.

Furlanetto ▶ G

San Polo 2768b, Calle dei Nomboli, +39
041 5209544, closed Saturday and Sunday
(8.30 am–1 pm and 2.30 pm–6 pm)

In this narrow but much
frequented *calle*, Franco
Furlanetto plies his trade. If you
don't need a *fòrcola* just at the
moment, you can peek inside
and watch him at work, or leaf
through a gondola-related
publication.

Brandolisio ▶ I

Castello 4725, Sotoportego Corte Rota,
+39 041 5224155, closed Saturday and
Sunday (9.30 am–1 pm and
3.30 pm–7 pm)

This was once the workshop
of the master oarmaker Carli,
and the atmosphere is still
amazing.
To call Paolo a man of few
words would be a gross
understatement, but that is
immaterial.
His *fòrcole* do all the talking.

Spazio Legno ▶ T

Giudecca 213b, Area Cantieristica Minore, +39 041 2775505,
closed Saturday and Sunday (8.30 am–12.30 pm and 1.30 pm–6 pm)

The generous 800 square-metre site enables you to
browse at leisure through some weird and wonderful
constructions. There's furniture made to order or from
drawings, doors, windows, hanging gardens and *altane*,
the typical Venetian roof gardens. You won't find it easy to
face down Aldo, Stefano, Damiano or Ignazio. They have
worked with all the most infuriatingly nit-picking designers
in the Venice area, and they have always come out on
top. Their love of tradition and state-of-the-art equipment
means they are also in demand with clients from
abroad. Not bad going in a city that is haemorrhaging
manufacturers.

Gilberto Penzo ▶ F

San Polo 2681, Calle Seconda dei Saoneri, +39 041 719372,
closed Sunday (9 am–1 pm and 2 pm–6 pm)

If you find the shop door closed, try on the left
a few metres further on. You'll probably find
Gilberto Penzo in his studio, designing a boat
of some kind. This is where you should come
if you have always loved model ships, yachts
or just rowing boats, built with a craftsman's
meticulous care.

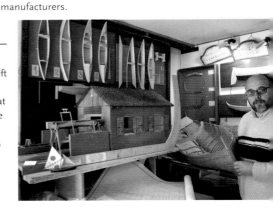

You'll find all you need in this atmospheric
shop, redolent of wood and glue. There are
also naval models, plans, construction kits,
reliefs of historic constructions, *fòrcole* and
votive offerings made by seafarers.

Dalla Venezia ▶ G

San Polo 2204, Calle del Scalater, +39 041 721659, open all week and sometimes on Sunday (8 am–12.30 pm and 3 pm–7.30 pm)

As Angelo works away at his lathe, the objects he makes take on a polished, rounded shape.
He makes door handles, eggs, spheres, table legs, candleholders and supports for the glass balls
of local fortune tellers. Children he takes a shine to will receive one of his spinning tops. In beautifully
turned wood, of course.

De Marchi ▶N

San Marco 3157a, Piscina San Samuele, +39 041 5285694, closed Saturday and Sunday (9 am–12.30 pm and 1.30 pm–6 pm)

A celebrated, respected woodworker, many of whose works are exhibited in museums around the world, Livio De Marchi is the creator of much copied surrealist wooden sculptures in *cirmolo*, the interestingly knotty silver lime that grows on Alpine slopes. It is impossible to go through San Samuele without noticing his fascinating window display. Unlaced shoes, shirts hanging out to dry, socks, vests, and suitcases are all carved in natural colour wood. Recently, Livio has been designing objects in other materials, but hanging wooden jackets (€ 6-7,000) are still his forte. Occasionally, you can catch him "driving" his sporty pride and joy along the city's canals.

–99

Fabbro ▶H

San Polo, Ruga Vecchia San Giovanni, no telephone, open almost every day (10.30 am–6 pm)

The Fabbro family's cart has been sitting in the *calle* since the 1940s. It brims with wooden objects, including handmade items from Carnia, constructed by the few ageing craft workers who still remember how to do so. There are spoons, ladles, spatulas and the lovely baling scoops that some boat-deprived bar owners have turned into eye-catching breadbins.

Barbon ▶F

San Polo 2856, Calle dei Calegheri, +39 041 5222312, closed Saturday afternoon and Sunday (7.30 am–12.45 pm and 3 pm–6.30 pm)

Bruno Barbon is a marvellous carver. He makes mirrors, frames mainly to order, angry-looking lions of Saint Mark and is also the last woodworker in Venice to make the celebrated *moretti*, or blackamoors.

gondolas

What if you want to buy a gondola? There are very few *squeri* (boatyards) left to pass on this ancient, but constantly renewed, art. Over the centuries, gondolas have changed their appearance and proportions. Today, a gondola is about 10.80 metres long and about 1.40 metres wide. The detail that makes a gondola easily recognisable is the *ferro*, the complicated, distinctive iron decoration and guard on the prow.

The hull is asymmetrical to facilitate rowing with a single oar, positioned towards the stern on the starboard side. The oar gains leverage from a wooden rowlock known as a *fòrcola* and is handled by the gondolier, who stands facing the prow

on a surface made up of a complicated arrangement of panels. One accessory that is no longer used is the *fèlze*, the removable cabin that was placed in the middle of the gondola to protect passengers from the cold and bad weather. A few years ago, an association named after the *El Fèlze* was set up for all the artisans who contribute to gondola building (www.elfelze.com). The group organises occasional visits to workshops.

Tramontin ▶ M

Dorsoduro 1542, Ponte Sartorio, +39 041 5237762, visits by appointment

This is the most venerable of Venice's *squeri*. The current owner's great-grandfather invented several of the gondola's components, which today are considered mandatory features. Roberto Tramontin uses traditional materials and techniques, including the traditional Venetian unit of measurement, the foot, equivalent to 34.7735 centimetres. Naturally, he is the despair of standardisers everywhere. Roberto is more than willing to welcome visitors who book ahead.

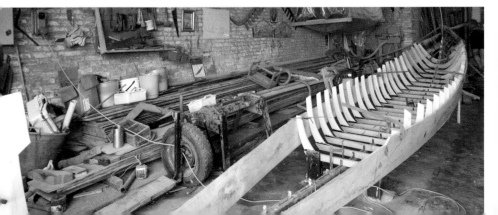

Bonaldo ▶ M

Dorsoduro 1545, Calle Balastro, +39 041 5236673

The roughest of the gondola-making diamonds. The owner acquired extensive experience with carpenters of the old school.

Crea ▶ T

Giudecca 212, Area Cantieristica Minore, +39 041 5231798

Gianfranco Vianello, nicknamed "Crea", began building Venetian vessels after a long and successful career as a regatta yachtsman.

Dei Rossi ▶ T

Giudecca 866a, Area Cantieristica Minore, +39 041 5223614

Although young, Roberto Dei Rossi has a very sensitive touch with traditional techniques and makes gondolas in the time-honoured fashion.

Della Toffola ▶ N

Dorsoduro 1097, San Trovaso, +39 338 3451116

The youngest gondola artisan, and a favourite with the older hands. The boatyard is in a very prominent position. Its characteristic Alpine architecture is courtesy of the mountaineers from Cadore and Val Zoldana who built it, having accompanied logs along the river route to Venice. It is beyond doubt the most photographed *squero* in the city and a magnet for tourists.

Canaletto ▶ D

Cannaregio 6301, Rio dei Mendicanti, +39 041 2413963

In Rio dei Mendicanti, the ancient *squero* immortalised by Canaletto in one of his early paintings is where Tom Price, a young man from North Carolina, makes his gondolas. He seems to have learned the ancient secrets of how the vessel is made in the space of just a few months. As a true American with a practical turn of mind, Tom has put together an impressive portfolio of customers in the United States. There are plenty of millionaires who want a real gondola to show off to their friends.

glass

First of all, go to the glass museum at Murano and see the Roman blown glass vases and 1st century BC murrines. The same technique is used by Murano's master glassmakers, who continue to make transverse incisions in multicoloured glass rods that have been fused together in various patterns.

The ancient glassmaking techniques are used by today's finest artisans. They adopt the same colours and the same shapes for their vases and glasses in the lagoon's nuanced greens, sky blues, ochres and pale ambers. Only the most expert master glassmakers know how to produce all the shades of red and yellow. Yet modern, linear design with its intense colour combinations also produces extraordinary articles, frequently the result of collaboration between well-known artists and master glassmakers.

For example, Egidio Costantini has worked with Picasso, Ernst, Chagall, Cocteau, Braque, Moore and Le Corbusier, turning glassmaking into a medium for the expression of modern art. If you do not plan to spend a fortune, you will still be able to afford some of the authentic objects on sale, such as the attractive *goti de fornasa* (literally, "kiln drops") in bright colours and interesting shapes.

Venini ▶ H

San Marco 314, Piazzetta dei Leoncini, +39 041 5224045, open all week, often also on Sunday (9.30 am–7.30 pm)
Many well-known architects and designers have worked with Venini. The legacy from this is an attractive exhibition of contemporary art, with works by Gae Aulenti, Giò Ponti, Vico Magistretti, Ettore Sottsass, Carlo and Tobia Scarpa and Tapio Wirkala, to mention just a few. The new owners have perked up the range by calling in new designers.

Pauly & C. — Compagnia di Venezia e Murano ▶I

San Marco 4391a, Calle Larga San Marco, +39 041 5209899, open all week (10 am–6 pm)

This is the place to come for a major purchase. Direct sales from the factory and a substantial turn over ensure value for money, even on top-of-the-range items, as connoisseurs are well aware. On request, they will show you the sample collection, in other words almost 2,000 square metres where you will find lamps three metres in diameter, sophisticated filigree cups, carafes, chalices and centrepieces for princely tables. Table services can be made to order. The customer portfolio includes almost all the world's noble houses. Like all rich people, royals know where to get a bargain. Still, not to worry. There is plenty of great stuff at affordable prices.

Barovier ▶N

San Marco 3216, Calle delle Carrozze, +39 041 5226102,
closed Sunday and Monday (9.30 am–12.30 pm and 3.30 pm–7.30 pm)

Marina Barovier has promoted some of the leading designers of contemporary Murano glass, such as Carlo Scarpa and Napoleone Martinuzzi. The exhibition space includes classic floral murrine vases by Barovier favourites, pieces by great early 19th-century designers and a by few contemporary artists. Prices go from € 4-40,000.

L'Isola ▶o

San Marco 1468, Campo San Moisè, +39 041 5231973, open all week (9 am–7 pm, only from January to March 9 am–1 and 3.30 pm–7 pm and closed Sunday)

This is where you will find the glassware of brothers Carlo and Giovanni Moretti in an atmospheric iron and wood display. The range combines the ancient skills of Murano's master glassmakers, in this case a family tradition, with the insights of contemporary Italian design. The vases, and especially glasses, in limited-production Murano glass have been selected for display in the world's leading museums.
We need only mention the *Cartoccio* vase or the *Ottagonale* glass, or the generous range of collectable *Calici* (€ 216) that have now become classics.

Micheluzzi ▶N

Dorsoduro 1071, Ponte de le Maravegie, +39 041 5282190, +39 041 5232856, closed Sunday and Monday (10.30 am–12.45 pm and 3 pm–6.30 pm)

For his murrine vases, Massimo Micheluzzi favours red, black and blue that he grinds to an intense saturation. The graphic, and on occasion almost organic, patterns make surfaces that resemble magnified marine life forms.
Prices range from € 1,500-3,500.

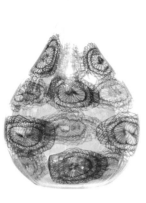

Belus ▶ N

Dorsoduro 369, Fondamenta de l'Ospedaletto, + 39 041 5234881, closed Tuesday (12 am–6 pm)

A small gallery where you will find glasses and vases created by Orlando Zennaro and his son, Stefano, using the filigree technique. Design is in the capable hands of Daniela Zentilin.

L'Angolo del Passato ▶ N

Dorsoduro 3276, Campiello dei Squelini, +39 041 5287896, closed Sunday (9.30 am–12 pm and 4 pm–7 pm)

Giordana Naccari is as Venetian as they come. Her shop is popular with other locals for its original merchandise and affordable prices. You'll find antiques, modern collectables, 20th-century glass, objets d'art and curios. There is a fine range of glasses, including Marie Brandolini's brightly coloured *Goti* (€ 50).

Sent ▶ N

Dorsoduro 669, Campo San Vio, +39 041 5208136, open all week (10 am–6 pm)

Marina and Susanna Sent have a nice line in necklaces (€ 20-200) made from pieces of glass on steel wire or leather. Discriminating designers are among their clientele.

The Sents also have Ivan Bai vases, inspired by shapes from nature.

Orsoni ▶ A

Cannaregio 1045, Sotoportego dei Vedei, +39 041 2440002-3, visits by appointment

In Venice, Orsoni is synonymous with mosaic. Orsonis have been working enamel and gold for four generations. Today, the business is run by a non-Venetian company but the original Orsoni technicians and craft workers have stayed on. Large plates are handled in the "colour library" before being cut into strips with a diamond blade. The strips are then cut into rectangles with hand shears. Mosaic tessarae are on sale in 3,000 different shades to retail, as well as trade, customers (€ 15 a kilogram for enamel, € 75 for gold). Courses are organised in the theory and practice of mosaics. Students spend a week in this house-cum-workshop, supervised by master mosaicists, to learn about the expressive potential of this marvellous medium.

Take a blowtorch and over the flame, melt variously coloured glass paste. Then with the aid of only a pair of long tweezers, shape insects, birds, small animals and figures. Impossible? There are just two masters of this sophisticated technique.

Murrina glassmaking involves joining different-coloured layers or rods of glass to create a pattern. The resulting base is heated and drawn out into a rod of the desired diameter. The rod is then cut up into a series of small discs. These are rearranged and heated again until they fuse together. Otherwise, they may be fused onto a glass base and used to make *perle* or blown articles.

Amadi ► G

San Polo 2747, Calle Saoneri, +39 041 5238089, closed Sunday (9.30 am–1 pm and 2 pm–6.30 pm, closed Saturday afternoon in summer)

Bruno Amadi is much loved by those who understand glass. Somehow, he manages to imbue every tiny item – whether it is a lettuce or a swan – with poetry. He also creates lagoon waterfowl, beans and irresistible dogs and cats.

Costantini ► C

Cannaregio 5311, Calle del Fumo, +39 041 5222265, closed Sunday (9.15 am–1 pm and 2.15 pm–6 pm)

Vittorio Costantini is the master of lampwork glass.
As if by magic, his blowtorch fashions insects, butterflies, birds, fish and precise replicas of the lagoon's flora and fauna. His skill and meticulous craftsmanship create tiny masterpieces that are authentic – and easy to pack – souvenirs of Venice.

ceramics

Imports of tableware, and often craftsmen, from the orient, Byzantium, North Africa and Spain created a desire to copy the colours and decorations on bowls, beakers, plates, ceramic tiles and majolica.

This love of soft, ductile clay, and of colours that reveal themselves only after firing, is still very much alive. Evidence is there in the many new studios set up by young people who have fallen in love with this ancient technique, and an art that blossoms into a myriad shapes and colours in their hands.

The ancient guild of Venetian ceramists has been reconstituted. Each year, the annual *Bochaleri in Campo della Bragora* exhibition is held, in collaboration with the Franchetti Collection at Ca' d'Oro and the students of the Carmini art school.

Arca ▶ G

Santa Croce 1811, Calle del Tentor, +39 041 710427, open all week, often also on Sunday (9.30 am–8 pm)

Teresa is always to be found here, painting her favourite Mediterranean red and blue enamels. She makes tiles (€ 10-30) that can be used indoors or outside, as well as large plates (€ 30-70), bowls (€ 14) and pot-bellied terra cotta vases that make attractive furnishing accessories. Articles can be made to order.

La Bottega degli Angeli ▶ G

San Polo 2224, Calle del Cristo, +39 041 710866,
closed Monday (10 am–1 pm and 3 pm–7.30 pm)

Silvia makes small objects, such as vases
or eye-catching terra cotta pendants. She
also enamels large vases and centrepiece
plates with her marvellous inborn sense
of colour.

Fustat ▶ M

Dorsoduro 2904, Campo Santa Margherita, +39 041
5238504, closed Saturday and Sunday (9.30 am–4 pm)

There is an atmosphere of enthusiasm
in the workshop of Cinzia Cingolani, who
divides her time between making pottery
and organising courses.

La Margherita ▶G

Santa Croce 2345, Sotoportego de la Siora Bettina, +39 041 723120, closed Sunday (9.30 am–7.30 pm)

Margherita Rossetto uses the majolica technique to transform everyday terra cotta into sunny, joyful objets d'art. She crafts coffee cups (€ 13), soap holders (€ 15) and chunky, practical mugs (€ 13).

Sabbie e Nebbie ▶G

San Polo 2768a, Calle dei Nomboli, +39 041 719073, closed Sunday (10 am–12.30 pm and 4 pm–7.30 pm)

Maria Teresa Laghi offers a range of deceptively simple, clean-lined articles. They're the sort of thing we call Japanese style, and the Japanese call Italian. There are Rina Menardi stoneware bowls and vases, cast-iron and porcelain Japanese teapots, not to mention Marcello Chiarenza's mysterious sculpted candleholders.

Madera ▶ M

Dorsoduro 2762, Campo San Barnaba, +39 041 5224181, closed Sunday (10.30 am–1 pm and 3.30 pm–7.30 pm)

If you like sparsely furnished homes that are a little Japanese and a little Scandinavian, with just a few ornaments in nature-inspired shapes, then Francesca Meratti is your woman. Browse her lamps, bowls, plates and hand-carved wooden spoons.

metalworking

Blacksmiths were the first artisans to form a guild. It was established around the year AD 1000 and in the late 18th century, there were more than 200 smithies, many located near the street that is still known as *Calle dei Fabbri*.

Much wrought iron is still made in Venice, but brass, bronze and silver are also worked to make eye-catching articles in the time-honoured manner, using traditional techniques. There are handles, knobs, bells, paperweights, name plates, lights, lamps, studs, door and drawer handles, candelabra, stands for lamps and street lamps, wall lights, hat stands, railings, gates, doors – often portraying the lion of Saint Mark, blackamoors, animal heads or cherubs – and window grills.

Ervas – Artistica Ferro ▶ G

Santa Croce 2137, Calle Longa, +39 041 5200490, closed Sunday and Monday (9 am–7 pm, Tuesday and Thursday 5 pm closing)

The Ervas family makes wrought – never pressed! – iron objects. In the shop, you will find ready made or specially commissioned curtain rods (€ 110-150), menacing-looking toasting forks (€ 50) and restored antique or imitation ironwork. They will also make keys for locks if you have lost the original.

Valese ►H, B

shop San Marco 793, Calle Fiubera, +39 041 5227282,
closed Sunday (10.30 am–7.30 pm)
foundry Cannaregio 3535, Madonna dell'Orto,
+39 041 720234, visits by appointment

Mario Valese bubbles with the enthusiasm
of someone who loves his work, despite
its extreme physical challenges.
He will tell you about the heat of
the foundry, the magical marriage
of zinc and copper fusing into
bronze, the incandescent liquids
– sometimes gold, silver or
copper – being poured into the
dies, some dating from the 18th
century, and the objects that
finally take shape.

His shop in the heart of the city is
run by his formidable elder sister
Loredana, who has always looked
after public relations and knows
everyone who is anyone in Venice.
Door knobs and handles,
made to order if necessary, cost
€ 200-300. There are 60 different
models of gondola horse, and
impressive-looking door knockers.

If you get the
impression that you
are being watched
as you stroll round
Venice's *calli*, don't
worry. It's just the
musi da portòn
(literally "door
faces"). These
traditional door
knockers are often
in the shape of a
fierce-looking lion's
head with the knocker
clenched in its teeth.

Rossettin ▶ N

Dorsoduro 3220, Calle delle Botteghe, +39 041 5224195, closed Sunday (9 am–1 pm and 2.30 pm–7 pm)

Diego is a third-generation member of the Rossettin brass, bronze and copper working clan.
He turns metal into door and window handles, keyholes, gondola horses and bathroom accessories, to order or in reproduction.

Mazzucco ▶ L

Castello 3800, Calle del Dose, +39 041 5236079, closed Saturday and Sunday (9 am–12.30 pm and 3.30 pm–7 pm)

A creative engraver. Inspiration comes from articles displayed in Venice's museums for unique, hand-crafted objects made using traditional techniques. Cups, candelabra and centrepieces are joined by frames, sugar bowls, tureens, spice holders, salt cellars, amulets, mirrors, perfume holders and lamps.

De Rossi ▶ D, H

forge Cannaregio 5045, Calle del Fumo,
+39 041 5200077, closed Saturday and Sunday
(8.30 am–12.30 pm and 2.30 pm–6.30 pm)
shop Cannaregio 4311, Strada Nuova,
+39 041 5222436, open all week
(9.30 am–1 pm and 2.30 pm–6.30 pm)

The typical Venetian lanterns are
bubbles of glass blown inside an iron
cage. Just one is sufficient to create
lagoon atmosphere. This is where
you can find around 50 different
models in an endless range of
colours (from € 60).

Lena ▶ H

Castello 5919, Salizada San Canzian, +39 041 5237478,
closed Sunday (9 am–12.30 pm and 4 pm–7.30 pm)

When high water reaches 90 centimetres,
Franco Barisoni has to work in rubber
boots, but it takes more than this to
upset him. Franco is a knife grinder.
He'll sharpen your knives
or scissors, and also has
a fine selection of cutlery,
including tweezers to
descale raw fish, forks and
pincers for eating lobster
and crab, Japanese ceramic
knives, lefthanded scissors
and rounded ones for clipping nose or ear hair.
There are professional barber's clippers, Swiss army knives
and yachting knifes with useful attachments for seafarers.

_115

Psalidi ▶ E

Santa Croce 360h, Rio Terà dei Pensieri, +39 041 711054, closed Saturday and Sunday
(8.30 am–12.30 pm and 2 pm–6 pm)

Architects from the nearby university
faculty bring their weirdest ideas
here to be clad in iron.
Today, Piero enthusiastically carries
on the family tradition, making
wrought-iron grills and gates.
This is also a good place to have
machine tools made or repaired.

paper

The paper industry really took off in Venice with the boom in printing during the 16th century. It was not just white paper for the presses. Parchment, superb-quality letter paper for the rich merchants of the east and west, and decorated binding papers were also produced.

We may be heading towards a virtual, paperless society, but paper itself still exercises enormous fascination. It is no coincidence that new shops continue to open for the sale of decorated paper mementoes of Venice. You'll find plenty of albums, briefcases, notebooks, frames and boxes large and small, not all of them particularly worthwhile.

Cartavenezia ▶ G

Santa Croce 2125, Calle Longa,
+39 041 5241283, closed Sunday
and Monday morning (11 am–1 pm
and 3.30 pm–7.30 pm)

Their varied experience in graphic design, paper and ceramics prompted Fernando and Zelda to develop their sophisticated cotton paper technique. The bas relief paper (€ 20-60) is a genuine tactile pleasure. The subjects range from the classic Venetian lion to cherubs, nymphs, angels, horses, peacocks and *patere*, the characteristic Byzantine or Romanesque bas relief tondos that you can see on the façades of Venetian palazzos. The paper is also used to cover albums (€ 45-85) and notebooks (€ 13-45).

Valese — Ebrû ▶ N

San Marco 3471, Campo Santo Stefano,
+39 041 5238830, open all week (10 am–7 pm)

Ebrû is a Turkish word that derives
from the Persian *ebri*, meaning
cloudy. It is also the name of an
ancient method of decorating paper
in different colours that mimic the
veining of stone or marble.
The swift movements of the craft
worker's hand "write" on a liquid surface,
forming patches, marblings and waves.
The coloured image that the sheet takes
up by absorbing the paint suspended
in the liquid is unique and unreplicable.
A few decades ago, Alberto Valese rediscovered
the ebrû technique, transforming it into a typically
Venetian product. In addition to the unique marbled sheets (€ 8),
his shop stocks other kinds of premium printed or glued paper,
Japanese suminagashi marbled paper (€ 13) and letter paper.
Don't forget to cast an eye over Alberto's printed silk accessories.
Elsewhere in the city, you will find many modest imitations of
Alberto's highly skilled work, on sale – incredibly – at higher prices.

Tagliapietra ▶I

Castello 3371a, Ponte de la Comenda, +39 041 5230641,
closed Sunday (8 am–1 pm and 3 pm–6.30 pm)

A small craft bookbinder, a stone's throw from the Scuola di San Giorgio
degli Schiavoni. On sale here are
albums, diaries and boxes covered
with Alberto Valese's marbled paper.

Pitacco ▶I

Castello 4758, Ruga Giuffa, +39 041 5208687, closed
Sunday (9 am–12 pm and 3 pm–8 pm)

Have you finally collected the whole
series of magazines? Do you want
to get a favourite old book bound?
Gianni Pitacco will do a superb job.

Olbi ▶C, H

gallery and workshop Cannaregio 5421/a, Calle Varisco, +39 041 5224057,
closed Saturday and Sunday (9 am–12.30 pm and 3 pm–6.30 pm)
shop Cannaregio 6061, Campo Santa Maria Nova, +39 041 5237655,
closed Sunday (10 am–12.30 pm and 3.30 pm–7.30 pm)

Paolo Olbi has been binding for more than 40 years.
His handiwork is impossible to confuse with the pale
imitations on sale in so many of the small shops scattered
around Venice. Paolo makes table and desktop articles
in marble paper or leather. Choose one of his
notebooks, albums or boxes if you want to give
a present in the finest binding tradition.
The new gallery features a display of the works
that Paolo has created in collaboration with
other Venetian artists and craft workers.

Carta da Cassetti ▶○

Dorsoduro 364, Campiello Barbaro, +39 041 5232804,
closed Sunday (10 am–6 pm)

Franco Cassetti lost his heart to printing on paper.
He uses old Pakistani wooden stamps, or new
ones in resin that he has engraved himself with
designs from mosaics, Venetian architecture or
fish. Sometimes, he colours freehand, using fresh
paint on a dry background, but he also uses gold
or copper on black. Now and again, he mixes
techniques and no one can predict what will
emerge. In a nutshell, this is where to come for
hand-printed sheets of paper (€ 12-20) to cover
boxes, or line drawers (the "casetti" of the shop's
and owner's name) if you prefer.

Polliero ▶F

San Polo 2995, Calle dei Frari, +39 041 5285130,
closed Sunday (10.30 am–1 pm and 3.30 pm–7.30 pm)

This long-established craft binder has a huge
selection of notebooks, books, boxes, and little
bureaux covered in marbled or glued paper, but
there are also superb leather bound albums for
your favourite photographs.

 **paints**

In a city that inspires professional painters, tourists and even artistically challenged Venetians to capture their emotions on a sheet of paper, there have always been plenty of art supply shops to give sketchers, artists and sculptors the requisites to reproduce the churches, palazzos and light reflected on the canals.

Accademia ▶ N

Dorsoduro 1044, Campiello Calbo, +39 041 5207086, closed Saturday afternoon and Sunday (9 am–1 pm and 2 pm–7 pm)

This is the stationer's used by students from the nearby Accademia, even though it has now moved to the Zattere. You'll find everything a budding artist could need.

Arcobaleno ▶ N

San Marco 3457, Calle delle Botteghe, +39 041 5236818, closed Sunday (9 am–12.30 pm and 3.30 pm–7.30 pm)

Perhaps better known as "Da Massimo" (Max's), the shop stocks solvents, cleaners, dyes and the most eye-catching wall of paints in the city.

Arte & Design ▶ F

Santa Croce 53a, Campiello Mosca, +39 041 710269, closed Sunday (8 am–1 pm and 3 pm–7.30 pm)

Some customers till call this "I Pierini", but the new owners have now made their mark on the shop that used to be run by the legendary Pierina. This stationer's is a favourite with architecture students because it has an extensive stock of paper, cardboard, felt pens and – not many people today use Indian ink – cartridges for printers and plotters.

Il Fontego dei Colori ▶ A

Cannaregio 2739, Fondamenta degli Ormesini, +39 041 2759588, closed Sunday (8 am–1 pm and 3 pm–7.45 pm)

Located in an area with a high proportion of art students, this popular little shop offers materials for restoring wood or stone, for gilding, découpage and painting, as well as brushes, paints, pigments and earths.

Artemisia ▶ F

San Polo 2589, Campiello Zen, +39 041 2440290, closed Sunday (10 am–1 pm and 3.30 pm–7.30 pm)

How can you resist those delightful little tins? Watercolours, brushes and bottles of ink line up with dusting paper, gold leaf, glue, paints, resins for fine arts and restoration, paste and water-base size for gilding, clay, paper for engravings, and a good selection of materials for model making in a young, lively ambience. The Artemisia also organises courses in drawing, painting, engraving and ceramics, which are sometimes held in English.

La Beppa ▶ L

Castello 3166, Salizada San Francesco della Vigna, +39 041 5226968, closed Sunday (7 am–7.30 pm)

Once, Venice was full of little shops where you could find almost anything. Since people have to walk everywhere, there was at least one such shop in each district. Nowadays, there seems to be more demand for masks and ice creams, so if you find a traditional store, you take note. La Beppa has every possible brand and variation of solvents, cleaners, sponges, clothes horses, brushes, cords and nails, as well as paints and natural pigments in liquid form or powder. There are hundreds of different colours to cater for even the most sophisticated artist or artisan.

De Gaspari ▶ E

Dorsoduro 3522, Calle de la Cereria, +39 041 717135, closed Saturday afternoon and Sunday (8 am–7 pm)

Here the formidable Pierina caters for all the needs of the aspiring architects who live in the area. She has many designer gifts, office and desk accessories, bags and clocks.

Testolini ▶ H

San Marco 1744–1748, Fondamenta Goldoni, +39 041 5229265, closed Sunday (9 am–7 pm)

The best-known city centre stationer's. The stock includes office goods, paper, printer cartridges, floppy disks and CDs for computers, notebooks, pens and desk accessories from big name, big price tag labels. The other shop is too neat and tidy to be true. It sells paints and brushes for all media, from oil to tempera, watercolour, fabric, glass, metal and so on.

toys and games

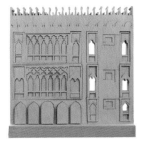

Zogàr a dama (play draughts), *a faraòn* (faro), *ai dai* (dice), *a le carte* (cards), *a la mora* (morra, a guessing game), *a sbaragìn* (a dice game), *zogàr de man* (to pull a fast one) and *zogàr de testa* (to rack one's brains). There are dozens of dialect expressions that bear witness to the love nurtured by Venetians old and young for games. There were plenty of outdoor games, like *massa e pindolo* (a baseball-like game played with broom handles), *cìmbani* ("bottle tops" used as missiles to strike a target) and *campanòn* (hopscotch). Today, these have been banned by the local authority, squeezed out by bar and restaurant tables and discouraged by the waste left by dogs with pooper scooper-deprived owners. Venice is a maze, making it the ideal place to dress up, switch roles, play hide-and-seek and generally not take yourself too seriously. A visit to the Correr Museum can be very instructive on the subject of traditional Venetian games. Here are some suggestions on where to find children's toys, ancient and modern.

Bambolandia ▶ G

San Polo 1462, Ponte de la Madoneta, +39 041 5207502, closed Sunday (9.30 am–12 pm and 1 pm–5.30 pm)

Beatrice Perini creates superb hand-crafted porcelain dolls. These artistic toys are either one-offs, or made in limited runs, mainly in biscuit porcelain.
The atmospheric shop-cum-workshop has a wide range of robots, huggable teddy bears and collectable wood and tin toys. Don't miss the clockwork ones. Nowadays, they are regarded as environment-friendly.

Il Baule Blu ▶F

San Polo 2916a, Campo San Tomà, +39 041 719448, closed Sunday
(10.30 am–12.30 pm and 4 pm–7.30 pm)

Give your new daughter one of these teddy bears and she will still be cuddling it when she is a teenager. Silvia Brinis and Claudia Grano make craft bears that are yours for € 40-250. Assembled and sewn entirely by hand using mohair, they are stuffed with straw or kapok and have glass eyes. The two owners also trade toys, so you can sometimes find collectable toy soldiers, tin trains or 1960s Barbie dolls.

Lanterna Magica ▶H

Castello 5379, Calle delle Bande, +39 041 5281902,
open all week (9 am–7.30 pm)

The New Age sounds, Scandinavian forests, waterfalls and wood puzzles may be of more interest to parents than children. Games and toys here are educational and intelligent, as are the scientific and natural curiosities. You'll see wooden trains, marionettes, toy soldiers, role games and construction kits. But there is also a medley of magic, conjurer's tricks, practical jokes and fluorescent sticks for the kids.

Signor Blum ▶M

Dorsoduro 2840, Campo San Barnaba, +39 041 5226367,
open all week (9 am–7.30 pm)

The simple, precise technique of stencilling and hand-painting – but with a big helping of imagination – produces these delightful puzzle pictures, cradle mobiles, clocks, interlocking animals, landscapes and Venetian scenes. The results are ravishing.

Venice Model Team ▶G

San Polo 2102a, Salizada San Polo, +39 041 710031, closed Sunday and Monday morning (10 am–1 pm and 3 pm–7.30 pm)

A paradise for boys of all ages. Model cars only. You'll find them in 1:43 (€ 4-50) and 1:18 (€ 19-120) scale that you can buy ready assembled or in kits, complete with accessories and decals. There are classic, Grand Prix and vintage models.

Also on sale are plastic construction kits of aeroplanes, tanks, trucks, model soldiers and cars, as well as a good range of spares and accessories for miniature four wheel drive fans.

Emporio Pettenello ▶F

Dorsoduro 2978, Campo Santa Margherita, +39 041 5231167, closed Sunday only in summer (9.30 am–1 pm and 3.30 pm–8 pm)

Wander through Campo Santa Margherita on any afternoon and you will see that this

is one of the most prolific parts of town. All those strollers, tricycles, footballs and chalks tell you why this generously stocked toy shop thrives, and why its staff are so well-informed on the latest fashions for the under-10s.

D.M. Venezia ▶H

San Marco 5545, Salizada del Fontego dei Turchi, +39 041 5222103, closed Sunday (10 am–7.30 pm)

This used to be one of the many souvenir shops, but Marino Marinoni's love of model making, coupled with the frustration of living in a city where the raw material is hard to come by, prompted him to transform the shop into a temple of miniatures, especially fantasy models.

There are hand-painted resin dragons (€ 15-80), Japanese manga comics, lead soldiers ready painted or in kit form, Warhammer 40000, accessories for making dioramas and the like, and a wide range of action figures, McFarlane toys, Magic, Yu-Gi-Oh, Pokemon and Soft Air cards.

photography

Venice is always posing. Every day, the city is the subject of millions of photos taken by the thousands of cameras being toted round the streets. Increasingly often, you bump – quite literally – into tourists looking at bridges, churches and palazzos through their camera lens. It is almost as if they need a filter to focus and frame the city's awesome beauty.

Everyone wants to take home a private image of Venice. It is fascinating to wander through the *calli* and *campielli* looking for a view, an angle or a magical shaft of sunlight. What are most captivating places? Well, the bell towers of Saint Mark's and San Giorgio Maggiore offer panoramic views. Dawn over the Fondamenta Nove is a favourite, as is sunset at the Zattere and the Ponte dei Miracoli. But watch out for the gondoliers. Not all of them are keen to be photographed.

Bianco Nero ▶C

Cannaregio 4559, Salizada del Pistor, +39 041 5228781, closed Sunday and Monday (9.30 am–12.30 pm)

If you're one of those people who love black and white photos, and rave about anyone who can still print them properly, possibly on fibre base paper, then Vittorio Pavan is your man. If you're looking for a souvenir a little different from the usual views, you can leaf through his catalogue and order a print of the film stars and international artists, captured during the golden age of the Venice film festival or just wandering around the *calli*. What about a Paul Newman or a Sophia Loren? Finally, if you are one of those people who have their own dark room, then you'll find a full range of developing and printing accessories.

 # prints

Since not everyone can afford a real work of art, whether it be a Canaletto
or merely a third-rate view painting, an engraving is a good cheaper option.
Engraving in Venice goes back to the late 15th century. In the 18th century,
the engravers formed their own guild, called the Arte degli Incisori,
to protect their exclusive right to the intellectual and economic property
of their work from imitations.
Chemicals, burins, presses, wood or copper plates, black inks, white paper,
precisely incised lines, shaded clouds, unexpected shafts of sunlight, alchemy
and mechanics all have a part to play in the magical world of engraving.

126_

Basso ►c

Cannaregio 5306, Calle del Fumo, +39 041 5234681, closed Saturday afternoon
and Sunday (8.30 am–12.30 pm and 2.30 pm–6.30 pm)

In his tiny printing shop, Gianni Basso makes business
cards (€ 55 for 100), bookplates (€ 50 for 100), letter paper
and invitations for customers all over the world.

Fallani ►C

Cannaregio 4875, Ponte dei Gesuiti,
+39 041 5235772, closed Sunday (7 am–1 pm),
visits by appointment

Artistic screen printing. Maestro
Fiorenzo Fallani puts his vast fund
of professional skill, acquired in
the course of a long career, at the
service of leading contemporary
artists.

Cattarin ►G

Santa Croce 2100, Calle della Chiesa,
+39 041 5240772, closed Sunday (3 pm–8 pm)

In line engraving, the ink penetrates a
mark cut into the metal, and the paper
has to be damp and absorbent to take
it up. Is that the secret of the softness
of Diego Cattarin's works?

Il Graffio ►M

Dorsoduro 3186,
Calle delle Botteghe,
+39 041 2413493, closed Sunday
(10.30 am–12.40 pm and 2.30
pm–7.30 pm)

Alessandra D'Agnolo and
her line-engraving press
produce exquisite artistic
prints using drypoint,
etching and aquatint
techniques.
Her Venetian prints are
attractive, but her own
creations are even more
interesting.
Creativity bursts from
Alessandra's every pore,
and you will find all sorts of
fascinating articles that she
has made in the shop.

Petra ▶○

San Marco 2424, Calle Larga XXII Marzo,
+39 041 5231815, open all week
(10 am–7.30 pm; Sunday closing 6 pm)

A large, very central shop with original
engravings from the 17th century on,
as well as nautical charts, historic maps
and views by Canaletto and Visentini.
There are also some fine contemporary
watercolours.

Scriba ▶F

 San Polo 3030, Campo dei Frari, +39 041 5236728, open all week
(9.30 am–7.30 pm, Sunday closing 6 pm)

In among the antiqued maps and giftware, you will find
atmospheric views of the lagoon (€ 350-3,000)
by Livio Ceschin, a young Treviso-born engraver who has
won a number of awards and is known all over the world.

Alchymia ▶M

Dorsoduro 2946, Campo Santa Margherita, +39 041 5236570,
closed Sunday (9.30 am–1 pm and 3.30 pm–5.30 pm)

Antonella Di Giacobbe produces wonderful line-engraved
prints on Venetian themes, to order if required.
They make wonderfully stylish invitations.
Her small printing works also sells inks and tools
for line engraving and wood engraving.

Bottega del Tintoretto ▶ B

Cannaregio 3400, Fondamenta dei Gesuiti, +39 041 722081, closed Sunday (10 am–7 pm)

A graphic studio and printing works in what during the 16th century was the home and workshop of Jacopo Robusti (1518-1594), better known as Tintoretto.

Roberto Mazzetto is the man behind the counter in this time capsule of a shop. Visitors come to find out about the techniques of traditional artistic printing, engraving, binding and lithography, as well as the experimental and empirical approaches developed by 20th-century artists.

Many famous names collaborate with Roberto. Established artists come to develop new graphic techniques and tools, or hone the manual skills needed to create their works.

Periodically, the shop organises cultural events, exhibitions, lectures, theoretical and practical courses and seminars to introduce and explore various techniques.

You can even stay here to complete your work.

The workshop has bed & breakfast apartments for the purpose.

📘 books

In the late 15th century, there were 200 printers in Venice. The city became the most important book centre in 16th-century Europe and two out of three books printed in Italy came from Venice. They were much sought after for the quality of the printing and the elegance of the binding. The city was a huge emporium of ideas, manual skills and book-related knowledge. The most celebrated printer was Aldus Manutius (Aldo Manuzio), who gained fame with his *Hypnerotomachia Poliphili*, an erotic allegory that was the forerunner of modern paperbacks.

The cult of books remains alive in the many bookshops of modern-day Venice, some specialising in particular market niches. Venetian booksellers tend to be grumpy *i sa tutto lori* (know-it-alls), but where would we be without them?

Bertoni ▶ H, G

San Marco 3637b, Rio Terà dei Assassini, +39 041 5229583, closed Sunday
(9 am–12.30 pm and 3 pm–7.30 pm)
San Marco 4718, Calle dei Fabbri, +39 041 5224615, closed Sunday
(9.30 am–1 pm and 3 pm–7.30 pm)

Secondhand books, remainders and a family that has been devoted to the trade for generations. The shop is narrow, dusty and as untidy as a warehouse, but with a little patience and a sharp eye, you can find superbly produced catalogues for major exhibitions at half price. The son of the family in Calle dei Fabbri sells mainly remainders.

Cafoscarina ▶ N

Dorsoduro 3225, Campiello dei Squelini, +39 041 5229602, closed Saturday and Sunday (9 am–6 pm)
Dorsoduro 3259, Campiello dei Squelini, +39 041 5229602, closed Sunday (9 am–7 pm, Saturday 9 am–12.30 pm)

Two bookshops with two souls, one scientific and the other arts-oriented. Economics, IT, law, mathematics, chemistry and environmental science in one, and in the other a selection of literature and quality non-fiction titles that is unrivalled in Venice. A glance at the window display is useful guide to what you might find in the often-overcrowded interior.

al Capitello ►C

Cannaregio 3762, Calle Racchetta, +39 041 5222314, closed Sunday
(9 am–12.30 pm and 3.30 pm–7.30 pm)

A while ago, Antonio Mazzucco took over this bookshop previously
known as a supplier of school textbooks, dictionaries and atlases.
Today, there is a section that betrays the new
owner's passion for mountaineering.

Cluva ►E

Santa Croce 191, Tolentini, +39 041 5226910,
closed Saturday and Sunday (9 am–6 pm)

Situated inside the former home of the
University of Venice Institute of Architecture,
whose entrance was designed by Carlo Scarpa,
Cluva specialises in architecture texts and
journals. It is popular with students and
professional architects, interior designers,
furnishers, surveyors and engineers.

Emiliana ►H

San Marco 4487, Calle Goldoni, +39 041 5220793, open all week
(10.30 am–1 pm and 2 pm–7 pm)

A shop that caters mainly for tourists of the more cultured
variety. The stock includes Venetian-themed photobooks
and guide books in various languages.
There are also a few old books.

Fantoni Libri Arte ►H

San Marco 4119, Salizada San Luca, +39 041 5220700,
closed Sunday (10 am–8 pm)

The name is the same, but over the past few years
new owners Gabriella and Edoardo have expanded
the clientele while conserving the ambience a refined
bookshop that specialises in ancient and modern
art, graphic design, architecture and photography,
including foreign and rare books, catalogues and
journals. This is an Aladdin's cave for anyone
interested in illustrated books.

Filippi ►H

Castello 5763, Castello del Paradiso, +39 041 5235635, closed Sunday (9 am–12.30 pm and 3 pm–7.30 pm)
Castello 5284, Casseleria, +39 041 5236916, closed Sunday (9 am–12.30 pm and 3 pm–7.30 pm)

A bookshop and publisher with a fine tradition and a consuming
passion for anything Venice-related, including history and art history.
The last surviving craft publisher.

Giunti Al Punto ▶ G, A

San Polo 1128, Campo Sant'Aponal, +39 041 5208760, open all week (9 am–8 pm, Tuesday and Friday opening 10 am)
Cannaregio 282, Campo San Geremia, +39 041 2750152, open all week (9 am–12 am)

Two large bookshops with all the latest books, topsellers, a good range of guides and a fair selection of children's books. They deserve credit for their extended opening hours and young, tolerant staff.

La Ginestra ▶ H

San Marco 4995, Calle delle Acque, +39 041 2410705, closed Thursday afternoon
(10 am–12 pm and 3 pm–8 pm)

Perhaps the smallest bookshop in town, La Ginestra once specialised in anthropology, psychology and theatre. Today, it concentrates on erotic publications, poetry, short stories, cartoons and photobooks.

Goldoni ▶ H

San Marco 4742, Calle dei Fabbri, +39 041 5222384–5239736, closed Sunday (9.30 am–7.30 pm)

In every town in Italy, there is bookshop that people love – and hate – because it has a bit of everything. In Venice, it is the Goldoni, on whose two floors you can find anything from fiction, manuals and computer books to the Greek classics.

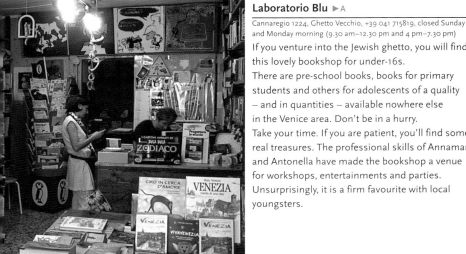

Laboratorio Blu ▶ A

Cannaregio 1224, Ghetto Vecchio, +39 041 715819, closed Sunday and Monday morning (9.30 am–12.30 pm and 4 pm–7.30 pm)

If you venture into the Jewish ghetto, you will find this lovely bookshop for under-16s.

There are pre-school books, books for primary students and others for adolescents of a quality – and in quantities – available nowhere else in the Venice area. Don't be in a hurry.

Take your time. If you are patient, you'll find some real treasures. The professional skills of Annamaria and Antonella have made the bookshop a venue for workshops, entertainments and parties. Unsurprisingly, it is a firm favourite with local youngsters.

Librairie Française ►I

Castello 6358, Barbaria de le Tole, +39 041 5229659, closed Sunday and Monday morning
(9 am–12.30 pm and 3.30 pm–7.30 pm)

Located on a route particularly appreciated by erudite visitors
to Venice is a bookshop with an atmosphere
of yesteryear, and a particularly superior selection
of French-language books. This is predictable
since the owner is French, and quite capable
of producing a copy of any book published
on the far side of the Alps in very short order.

Libreria del Campo ►I

Dorsoduro 2943, Campo Santa Margherita, +39 041 5210624,
closed Sunday morning (9.30 am–12.30 pm and 3.30 pm–7.30 pm)

Ancely isn't new to this bookshop but not everyone knows that she has taken
over the business. She concentrates on large-format photobooks, painting,
architecture and film, her great passion. She sets one corner aside for
good-quality infants' and children's books to keep local mums happy.

Linea d'Acqua ►G

San Marco 3717d, Calle della Mandola, +39 041 5224030, closed Sunday
and Monday morning (10 am–1.30 pm and 3.30 pm–7.15 pm)

You can tell what this bookshop is about from its window display.
Art and local history abound. Venice is everywhere in books large,
small, old or rare. Inside, there is a special focus on Casanova
and 18th-century Venice.

Il Mangialibri ►I

Castello 6442a, Barbaria de le Tole,
+39 041 2413178, closed Sunday
(9 am–1 pm and 4 pm–7.30 pm)

A wealth of children's books in
a shop so small that you want to
hug it. The stock is mainly from
small, good publishers for small,
careful readers. One corner is dedicated to the purchase and sale of
secondhand baby clothes to combat the tide of consumerism.

Marco Polo ►H

Cannaregio 5886a, Calle del Teatro Malibran,
+39 041 5226343, closed Sunday (9.30 am–1 pm
and 3.30 pm–8 pm)

A recently opened bookshop for
globe-trotters. You'll find guidebooks,
maps and route planners to take
you anywhere you want to go.
Travel literature and a small cookery
section complete the range of books.
Obviously, this is a good place to look
for a guidebook to Venice.

Mare di Carta ▶ E

Santa Croce 222, Fondamenta dei Tolentini, +39 041 716304, closed Sunday
(9 am–1 pm and 3.30 pm–7.30 pm)

There had to be a specialist bookshop in Venice for sea
and lagoon-related publications. You'll find books, charts, novels
of the sea and everything else an old salt could wish for. Cristina
and Antonio are also much-respected publishers of sea-related works
like *Fórcole*, *Navigare in Laguna* and others.

Miracoli ▶ H

Cannaregio 6062, Campo Santa
Maria Nova, +39 041 5234060,
open all week (9 am–8.30 pm)

It's hard to resist the
temptation to dig something special out of the piles
of new and secondhand books heaped higgledy-piggledy
on boxes. Then if you sit on a bench in the *campo*,
Luigi will come over and lend you a copy of *Ondine
et Poisson-Chat* (Water-Nymph and Catfish), which
he has had translated into several languages.

Mondadori ▶ O

San Marco 1345, Salizada San Moisè, +39 041 5222193, open all week
(10 am–10 pm, Sunday 3 am–8 pm)

Although we love tiny bookshops with loads of
personality, we candidly admit that we have great hopes
for this recently opened three-floor bookstore, which
boasts its own events room for presentations, exhibitions
and debates. There are children's books, guidebooks
in English, French, German and Spanish, IT, heaps
of fiction, an internet point and a reading corner.

Old World Books ▶ A

Cannaregio 1190, Ponte del Ghetto Vecchio, +39 041 2759456,
closed Saturday and Sunday (10 am–1 pm and 3 pm–7 pm)

Although Italy has no tradition of buying or swapping
secondhand books, some time ago John Francis
Phillimore opened this pleasant corner for bargain
hunters and seekers after rare or out-of-print
editions. Sometimes you will find him here on a
Sunday afternoon, if he has nothing better to do.

Punto Einaudi ►F

San Polo 2593, Campiello Zen, +39 041 714035, closed Sunday
(9.30 am–12.30 pm and 3 pm–7.30 pm)

Every city has a branch of Einaudi. Venice's is long on
Electa editions, partly because the shop is near the
Elemond stalls that are present at all the local exhibitions.
There are tempting discounts on offer.

San Pantalon ►F

Dorsoduro 3950, Crosera San Pantalon, +39 041 5224436,
closed Sunday (9 am–1 pm and 3 pm–7.30 pm)

Well known as a cat bookshop, San Pantalon has under
new management combined its traditional sectors
(children's books, music and cats) with an extended
range of fiction.

Sansovino ►P

San Marco 84, Bacino Orseolo, +39 041 5222623,
open all week (9 am–7 pm)

Near the world's loveliest square you will
find mainly Venice-related publications
and lots of guidebooks, in Italian and
other languages. Above all, Sansovino
offers heavyweight art books and
catalogues from the city's exhibitions.

Solaris ►B

Cannaregio 2332, Rio Terà de la Maddalena, +39 041 5241098,
closed Sunday morning (10 am–12.30 pm and 4.30 pm–7.20 pm)

A respected bookshop that specialises in cartoons,
science fiction, horror and fantasy.
Don't be put off by appearances. At the back of the shop
is an Aladdin's cave for connoisseurs, with 15,000 titles,
of which 2,000 are DVDs. This is where to come for
science fiction publishers that other shops don't stock,
such as sfbc, Galaxy, Urania, Editrice Nord, Fannucci and
Shake, to name but a few.

Studium ▶I

San Marco 337, Calle Canonica, +39 041 5222382, open all week
(9 am–7.30 pm, Sunday 10 am–2 pm)

Just behind this Basilica of Saint Mark is this bookshop,
which belongs to the diocese of Venice. Books on the
city's religious art and history, Christianity and other
religions, as well as icons and prints, together with
children's books and a good selection of guides
and foreign-language books are all on offer in the midst
of the deafening bedlam of tourists.

Tarantola ▶H

San Marco 4268, Campo San Luca, +39 041 5223413,
closed Sunday (9 am–12.30 pm and 3 pm–7.30 pm)

A quick glance at the always up-to-date
window display is de rigueur after a coffee in
Campo San Luca. An interesting selection
of paperbacks of all kinds is combined with
a more traditional range.

Il Tempio di Iside ▶G

Santa Polo 2659a, Calle Moro Lin, +39 041 715498, open all week (10 am–1 pm and 4 pm–8 pm)

Fabiana enthusiastically runs the only remaining bookshop in Venice
dedicated to the esoteric arts. Note the fine collection of crystal balls,
pyramids and amulets. Alchemy, parapsychology, esotericism, astrology,
New Age music and fairy-tales, manuals for meditation and yoga, alternative
medicine, tarot, Freemasonry, Theosophy and the arts rub shoulders on the
shelves. Occultists of the world, this is your bookshop.

Toletta ▶N

Dorsoduro 1214, Sacca de la Toletta, +39 041 5232034,
closed Sunday morning (9.30 am–7.30 pm,
in summer 9.30 am–1 pm and 3.30 pm–7.30 pm)

The book addict's paradise. Remainders discounted by 30, 40 or 50%
from nearly all Italian publishers. A must-visit bookshop for Venetians
and non-residents alike. Next door is Toletta Studio, which specialises
in architecture, contemporary art, literature
and philosophy for the reading lists of the
city's universities. The more recent Cube
opposite is the place for posters, T-shirts,
music CDs and lots of guidebooks in Italian
and other languages.

Tribunale ▶H

San Polo 117, Calle della Sicurtà, +39 041 5227907, closed Saturday and Sunday
(9 am–1 pm and 4.30 pm–7.30 pm)

Everything legal, in the sense of statute books and other law-related
publications. Next door to the courts, of course.

🎵 music

With its silences, footfalls and the gentle lapping
of water, Venice is the spiritual home of music
and the arts of Eurterpe. Historically, the city has
always been music-friendly, and the home
of musical experimentation. The tradition goes
back to the Renaissance of madrigals, Gabrieli
and Monteverdi, the 18th century of Vivaldi,
Benedetto Marcello and Galuppi, and the
20th century of Malipero, Nono and Maderna,
continuing with contemporary composers
like Claudio Ambrosini.

Music publishing was also important, as was
the production of music in a vast entertainment industry
that could call on the labour and skills of carpenters, architects,
set designers and painters, people who sold candles during
musical and theatrical productions, costume designers and mask
makers as well as musicians, singers, actors and coaches.
Music continues to be made all over Venice.
Much of it is targeted at tourists, but if you ask around,
you will probably be able to dig out some intriguing events.

> The mandolin is associated not
> just with Neapolitan music and
> early 20th-century popular song.
> It has been widely played all
> over Italy for centuries.
> The **Venetian mandolin** appears
> in many paintings on display at
> the Gallerie dell'Accademia.
> Like the mandola and the Genoese,
> Lombard, Turinese, Brescian or
> Cremonese, Roman, Neapolitan
> and Sicilian mandolins, the
> Venetian version has its roots
> in the Islamic musical
> culture introduced
> to Europe by the
> Crusaders.

—137

Il Suono Improvviso ▶c

Cannaregio 3546, Fondamenta dell'Abbazia, +39 041 2750049, closed Saturday and Sunday (10 am–12 pm and 3 pm–6 pm)

A teaching workshop set up and run by Giannantonio De Vincenzo.
Trumpet, keyboards, piano, saxophone, singing, modern guitar, jazz guitar, drums, electric bass,
harmony workshops, jazz improvisation,
band music for pianists, singers, guitarists or
percussionists, musical theory and double bass.
If you see hundreds of musicians swarming all
over the city on a Sunday in June, don't worry.
It's just *Venezia Suona*, an event that in recent
years has attracted more than 10,000 musicians
of all genres, from rock to classical, jazz,
popular, band and choir music, to play
in the city's *campi* and *campielli*. The day often
ends with a collective performance.

Venice Research ▶ G

Santa Croce 2165, Calle della Chiesa, +39 339 5609637, visits by appointment

Italian musical instruments from the 18th to the 20th centuries are bought, sold, valued and restored here. Stefano Pio has also written authoritative books on string instrument making in Venice (*Liuteri and Sonadori. Venice 1750–1870*, 2002 and *Violin and Lute Makers of Venice 1640–1760*, 2004). A place no specialist should miss.

Trevisin ▶ M

Dorsoduro 2627, Calle Lunga San Barnaba, +39 041 2410202, closed Saturday afternoon and Sunday (9.30 am–12.30 pm and 3 pm–7 pm)

Francesco Trevisin has been around since he left his full-time job as a technician at the Fenice opera theatre. He has studied, he has worked at craft workshops all over Europe and now he can lay claim to the title of the city's only string instrument maker. He builds, repairs and restores all string or plucked instruments using 18th-century techniques.

Regazzo ▶ I

Castello 4700, Campo San Provolo, +39 041 5287350, closed Sunday and Monday morning (9 am–12.30 pm and 3 pm–7 pm)

A musical instrument store connected with the well-stocked Padua-based company of the same name. This means that anything you can't find will arrive in double-quick time, including electric and acoustic guitars, keyboards, tuners, drums kits, wind instruments. This is also the place for piano servicing, tuning, repairs, restoration and storage, and instrument hire for concerts.

Mille e Una Nota ▶G

San Polo 1235, Calle del Perdon, +39 041 5231822,
closed Sunday (9.30 am–1 and 3 pm–7.30 pm)

A small shop that welcomes
customers with all the courtesy and
cosseting attention of a bygone age.
Harps, ethnic instruments, to order
if required, teaching instruments,
concertinas, scores and teaching
programmes for children.

Tempio della Musica ▶H

San Marco 5368, Calle del Fontego dei Turchi, +39 041 5234552,
closed Sunday (9 am–7.30 pm)

A CD shop, with mainly jazz, classical and opera
music, as well as old French songs and piano music.

Discoland ▶M

Dorsoduro 2760, Campo San Barnaba, +39 041 5287229,
closed Sunday (10 am–1 pm and 3 pm–8 pm)

Don't be put off by the gruff
welcome. This is a great place to
come for CDs. Blues, acid jazz,
funk, rap, fusion, jazz, jazz rock,
ambient music and much more.

Vivaldi Store ▶H

San Marco 5537, Calle del Fontego dei Turchi, +39 041 5221343,
open all week (9.30 am–7.30 pm)

Everything Vivaldi-related you could ever want or imagine.
There are chocolates, sweets, pencils, notebooks, pencil boxes,
all rigorously Vivaldified. Naturally, you'll also find music CDs with
the complete works of the great man. But one corner of the shop
has a specialist selection of Venetian Renaissance, pre-Baroque
and Baroque music, featuring Gabrieli, Monteverdi, Albinoni,
Marcello, Galuppi and others. You will also find programmes
and tickets for almost every concert in the city at La Fenice,
Malibran or in Venice's many churches and *scuole*.

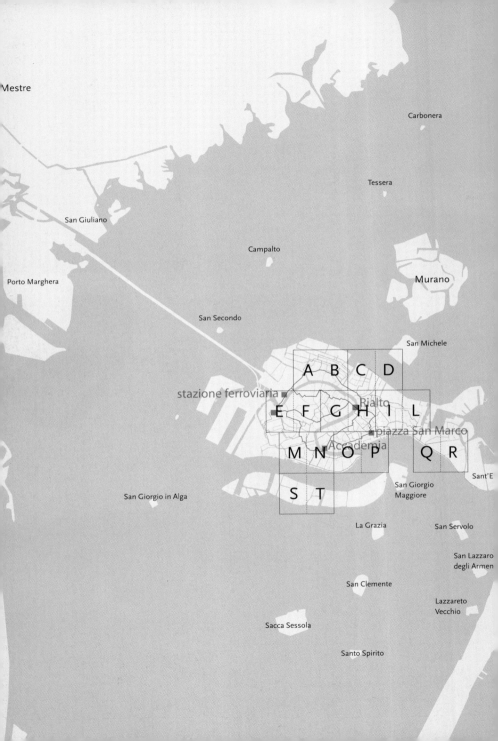

del Lovo

Torcello

Mazzorbo   Burano

San Francesco
del Deserto

San Giacomo
n Palude

Sant'Erasmo

Punta Sabbioni   Cavallino—Treporti

ignole

Lido di Venezia

maps

A

Cappuccine

f.ta della Sensa

f.ta di S. Girolamo

f.ta de le Capuzine

il Fontego
dei colori

f.ta dei Ormesini

Orsoni

campo del
Ghetto novo

Old World
Books

sinagoga
e museo ebraico

calle de le Chioverete

Laboratorio
Blu

f.ta de Cannaregio

sinagoga
spagnola

Volpe

Ghetto vecchio

Nobbe

f.ta Savorgnan

rio terà Frisetti

Marchi
Caffè
Costarica

Ca' Macana
atelier

Boutique
della Carne

Guglie

Martini

rio terà S. Leonardo

Boscolo

ponte delle Guglie

@

S. Leonardo

Giunti al punto

palazzo
Labia

S. Geremia

campiello
del Remer

S. Marcuola

dei Cavalletti

TRAGHETTO
S. MARCUOLA
7,45–13 (NO FESTIVI)
ESTATE 8–12,30

Fonda
dei Tur
(museo di
natura

Lista di Spagna

Biasio

@

Bevilacqua

Canal Grande

riva di Biasio

S. Zan Degolà

ponte degli Scalzi
(Miozzi 1934)

S. Simeon
Grando

lista vecchia dei Bari

F

Alaska

al Prosecco

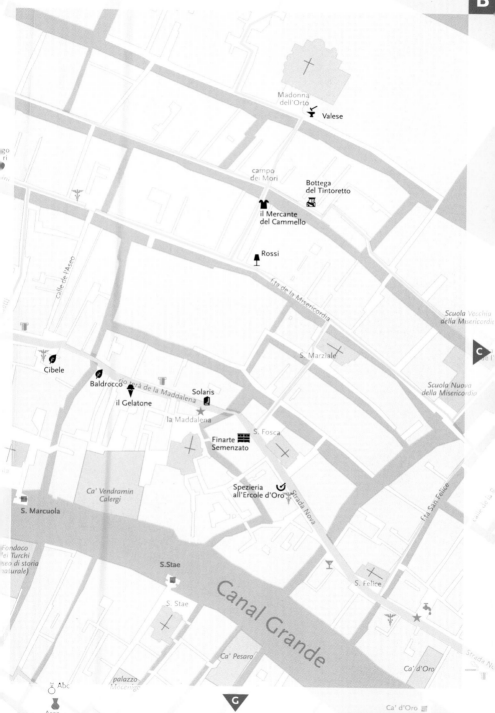

Madonna
dell'Orto

Valese

campo
dei Mori

Bottega
del Tintoretto

il Mercante
del Cammello

Rossi

f.ta de la Misericordia

Scuola Vecchia
della Misericordia

C

S. Marziale

Scuola Nuova
della Misericordia

Cibele

Baldrocco

o tera de la Maddalena

Solaris

il Gelatone

la Maddalena

Finarte
Semenzato

S. Fosca

Spezieria
all'Ercole d'Oro

Strada Nova

S. Marcuola

Ca' Vendramin
Calergi

f.ta San Felice

Fondaco
ei Turchi
seo di storia
naturale)

S.Stae

S. Felice

S. Stae

Canal Grande

Strada N

Ca' Pesaro

Ca' d'Oro

Abc

Arca

G

Ca' d'Oro

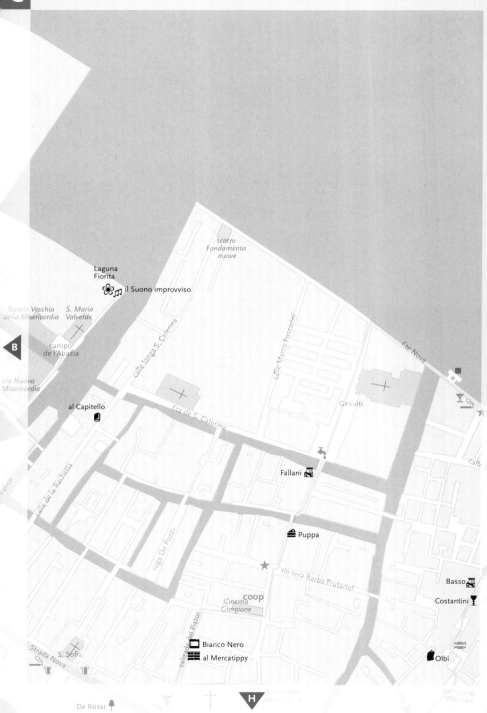

C

teatro
Fondamenta
nuove

Laguna
Fiorita

il Suono improvviso

Scuola Vecchia
della Misericordia

S. Maria
Valverde

campo
de l'Abazia

B

fte Nove

Calle Marco Foscarini

Calle longa S. Caterina

ola Nuova
Misericordia

Gesuiti

al Capitello

fta de S. Caterina

Fallani

Calle de la Racheta

Puppa

ruga Do Pozzi

rio terà Barba Frutariol

Basso

coop

Costantini

Cinema
Giorgione

salizada del Pistor

Bianco Nero

al Mercatippy

Olbi

Strada Nova

S. Sofia

De Rossi

H

gondola-ferry stops.
The Canal Grande can be crossed at seven
points in gondola-ferries for 40 cents.
The service is much patronised by Venetians

chemist's (9 am-12.30 pm and 3.45 pm-7.30 pm)
open on Saturday afternoon and Sunday on a rota system

fountain with drinking water

newsstand (7 am-6 pm)
open on Sunday on a rota system

traditional meeting place for an aperitif

fish stall
(Tuesday to Saturday, mornings only)

fruit and vegetable stall
(Tuesday to Saturday, mornings only)

flower stall
(Tuesday to Saturday, mornings only)

post office

token-operated laundry

ATM

cooperativa trasbagagli piazzale Roma
+39 041 5223590

left luggage
+39 041 5231107, open every day (6 am-9 pm)

coop   Coop supermarket

@   internet point

Fondamente Nuove

De Rossi

e larga dei Botteri

calle del Fumo

Canaletto

fte Nove

S. Lazzaro
ai Mendicanti

Ospedale Civile

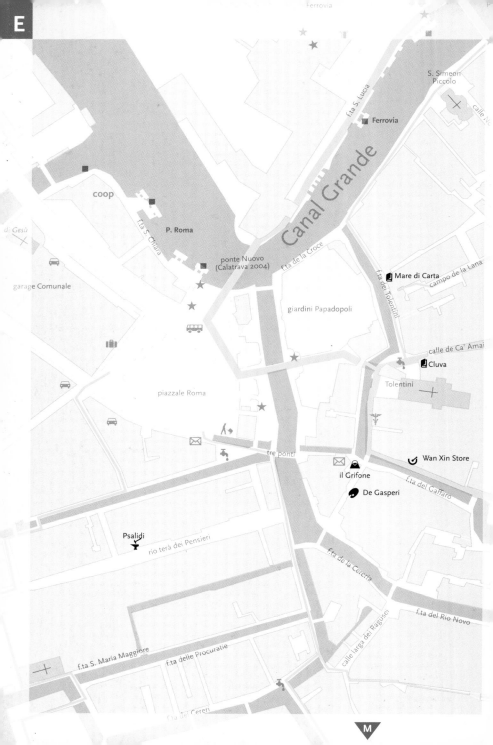

Ferrovia

S. Simeon
Piccolo

f.ta S. Luca

Ferrovia

calle N...

Canal Grande

coop

di Gesù

f.ta S. Chiara

P. Roma

ponte Nuovo
(Calatrava 2004)

f.ta de la Croce

f.ta del Tolentini

Mare di Carta

campo de la Lana

garage Comunale

giardini Papadopoli

calle de Ca' Amai

Cluva

Tolentini

piazzale Roma

tre ponti

Wan Xin Store

il Grifone

f.ta del Gaffaro

De Gasperi

Psalidi

rio terà dei Pensieri

f.ta de la Cereria

f.ta del Rio Novo

calle larga dei Ragusei

f.ta S. Maria Maggiore

f.ta delle Procuratie

f.ta dei Cereri

Alaska

Saraji Gallery

al Prosecco
coop
Rio Bio
S. Giacomo dall'Orio

campo Nazario Sauro

calle del Tentor

campo S. Boldo

Vio

f.ta Rio Marin

corte Canal

Trevisan

Buggio

Scuola Grande
S. Giovanni Evangelista

S. Stin

S. Agostin

calle delle Chiovere

a Mano

la Perlina

Punto Einaudi

Artemisia

Penzo

Frari

Longhi

Polliero

Cenerentola

il Te di Is

S. Rocco

campo Scuola Grande
Castelforte

salizada S. Pantalon

Tolin

San Rocco
Millevoglie
Scriba

Barbon

Tragicomica

casa
Goldoni
Mazzon – le Borse

Furl
Sabb

Arte & Design

campiello Mosca

Tonolo

San Pantalon

Zamattio

il Baule Blu
Cicogna

S. Toma

Miani

S. Pantalon

il Canapè

ponte de la Frescada

S. Toma

f.ta Malcanton

Emporio Pettenello

India

il Melograno

Cafoscarina

S. Margherita

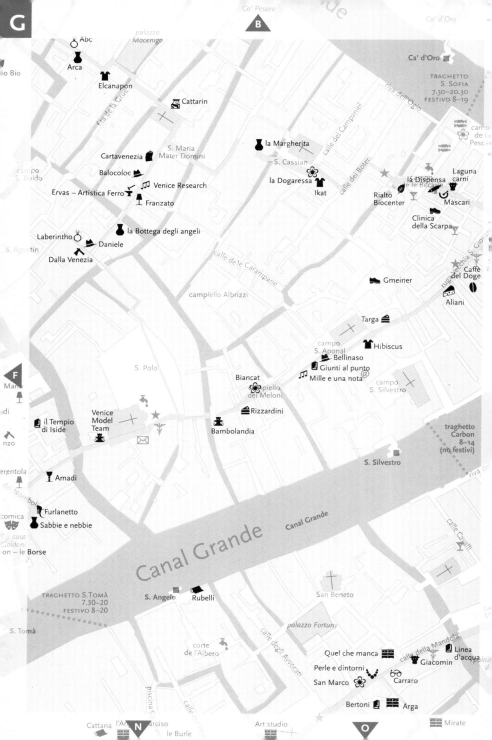

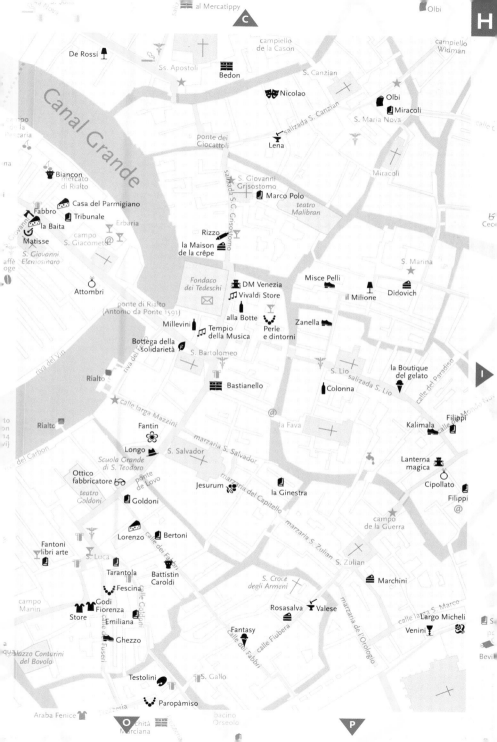

I

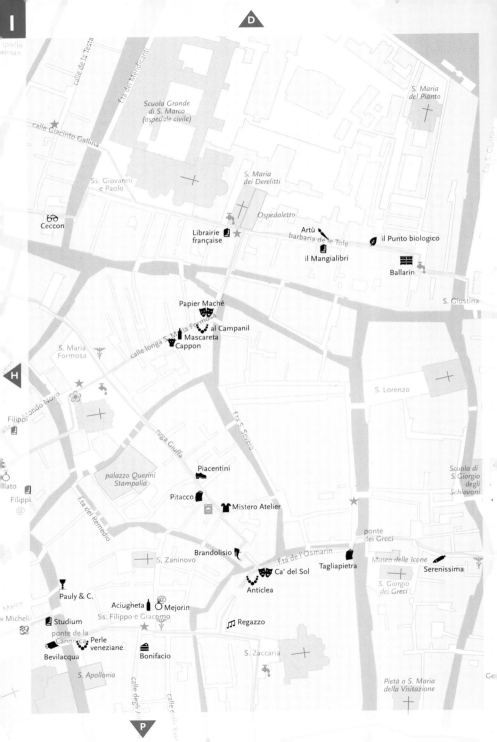

D

calle de la Testa

f.ta dei Mendicanti

S. Maria
del Pianto

Scuola Grande
di S. Marco
(ospedale civile)

calle Giacinto Gallina

Ss. Giovanni
e Paolo

S. Maria
dei Derelitti

Ceccon

Ospedaletto

Librairie
française

Artù
barbaria de le Tole

il Punto biologico

il Mangialibri

Ballarin

S. Giustina

Papier Maché

al Campanil

calle longa S. Maria Formosa

Mascareta
Cappon

S. Maria
Formosa

S. Lorenzo

H

alla Fondamenta Nova

Filippi

rruga Giuffa

f.ta S. Severo

Piacentini

palazzo Querini
Stampalia

Pitacco

Scuola di
S. Giorgio
degli
Schiavoni

lato

Filippi
@

Mistero Atelier

f.ta dei Remedio

ponte
dei Greci

Brandolisio

f.ta de l'Osmarin

Tagliapietra

Museo delle Icone

Serenissima

S. Zaninovo

Ca' del Sol

Anticlea

S. Giorgio
dei Greci

Pauly & C.

Aciugheta

Mejorin

Marco

Micheli

Studium

Regazzo

ponte de la
Canonica

Perle
veneziane

Bevilacqua

Bonifacio

Ss. Filippo e Giacomo

S. Zaccaria

S. Apollonia

calle degli

Pietà o S. Maria
della Visitazione

Ge

P

f.ta S. Giustina

Celestia

S. Francesco
della Vigna

Celestia

salizada S. Giustina

S. Ternita

la Beppa

S. Giovanni
di Malta

campo
delle Gate

campo
Do Pozzi

Vino e... vini
S. Antonin

Banco n. 10

S. Martin

campo
dell'Arsenale

campo
Bandiera e Moro

Gervasutti

S. Giovanni
in Bragora

Mazzucco

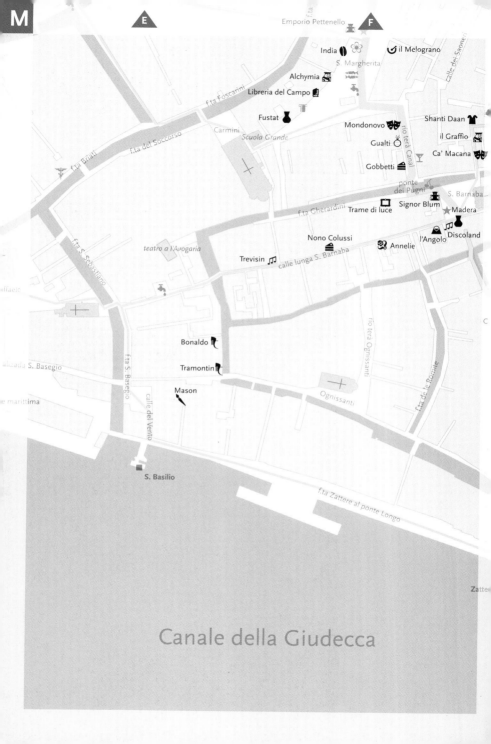

Emporio Pettenello

India

il Melograno

S. Margherita

Alchymia

Libreria del Campo

f.ta Foscarini

Fustat

Carmini

Scuola Grande

Mondonovo

Shanti Daan

il Graffio

Gualti

Ca' Macana

Gobbetti

rio terà Canal

ponte
dei Pugni

S. Barnaba

f.ta del Soccorso

f.ta Briati

Trame di luce

Signor Blum

Madera

f.ta Gherardini

l'Angolo

Discoland

Nono Colussi

Annelie

f.ta S. Sebastiano

teatro a l'Avogaria

Trevisin

calle lunga S. Barnaba

raffaele

Bonaldo

rio terà Ognissanti

f.ta le Romite

Tramontin

alzada S. Basegio

f.ta S. Basegio

Ognissanti

Mason

calle del Vento

e marittima

S. Basilio

f.ta Zattere al ponte Longo

Zatte

Canale della Giudecca

calle dei Saoneri

F   G   N

Cafoscarina
campiello
dei Squellini   Arras
l'Angolo del passato
Rossettin
Rillosi

Cattana   l'Angelo narciso
Ant. San Samuele   le Burle
veneziane
Antiquus   Arcobaleno   Valese – Ebrû
De Marchi
Barovier   Crovato   Zanutto
Kleine Galerie @

palazzo Grassi

salizada Malipiero

Ca' Rezzonico
S. Samuele
S. Samuele   S. Samuele

Ca' Rezzonico

S. Stefano

calle del Traghetto

TRAGHETTO
S. BARNABA
7.30–13.30
(NO FESTIVI)

Canal Grande

Fiorella Gallery

Cavalier

campo
Pisani

S. Vidal

Toletta
Canestrelli   Zaggia   Toletta
calle de la Toletta   Micheluzzi

Accademia

ponte dell'Accademia
(Miozzi 1933)

Canal Grande   O

Scarpa

rio terà de la Carità

Gallerie
dell'Accademia

Totem Gallery

Cantinone – già Schiavi
lo Squero
Accademia

campo
S. Vio

Mu
sho

Sent
Helene
Trevisanello

Ferr

S. Trovaso

Della Toffola

rio terà Antonio Foscarini

Pegg

S. Maria
della Visitazione

Gesuati   S. Agnese

da Nico

Zattere   f.ta Zattere ai Gesuati

Zattere

Rio terà

S

f.ta Zattere agli Incurabili

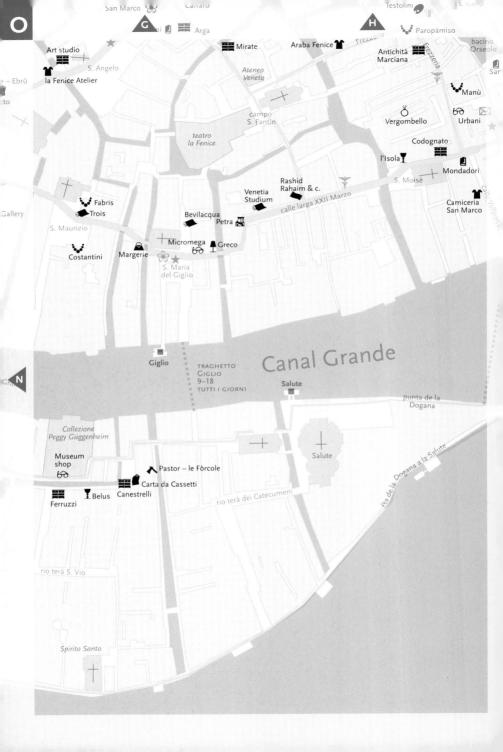

O

G Arga

H Paropàmiso

San Marco

Carraro

Testolini

S. Gallo

bacino
Orseolo

Mirate

Araba Fenice

Frezzeria

Antichità
Marciana

Sar

Art studio

la Fenice Atelier

S. Angelo

Ateneo
Veneto

Manù

campo
S. Fantin

Vergombello

Urbani

teatro
la Fenice

Codognato

l'Isola

Mondadori

S. Moisè

Camiceria
San Marco

Calle Vallaresso

Gallery

Fabris

Trois

S. Maurizio

Venetia
Studium

Rashid
Rahaim & c.

calle larga XXII Marzo

Bevilacqua

Petra

Costantini

Margerie

Micromega

Greco

S. Maria
del Giglio

Giglio

TRAGHETTO
GIGLIO
9–18
TUTTI I GIORNI

Canal Grande

Salute

punta de la
Dogana

N

Collezione
Peggy Guggenheim

Museum
shop

Salute

Pastor – le Fòrcole

Carta da Cassetti

Ferruzzi

Belus

Canestrelli

rio terà dei Catecumeni

Fta de la Dogana a la Salute

rio terà S. Vio

Spirito Santo

bacino
Orseolo

Sansovino

piazza S. Marco   campanile   palazzo Ducale

Albanesi

calle delle Rasse

ponte dei Sospiri

nù

ponte della Paglia

museo Correr   biblioteca Marciana

S. Zaccaria

el Todaro

ri

giardini ex Reali

Vallaresso

co

Vallaresso

TRAGHETTO DOGANA
9–14
TUTTI I GIORNI

bacino di San Marco

San Giorgio

fondazione Cini

R

campo
Ruga

f.ta di Quintavalle

f.ta de la Tana

S. Francesco
di Paola

f.ta S. Anna

Melita

ponte di Quintavalle

Seco Marina

f.ta S. Isepo

S. Isepo

Giardini

giardini della Biennale

riva dei Partigiani

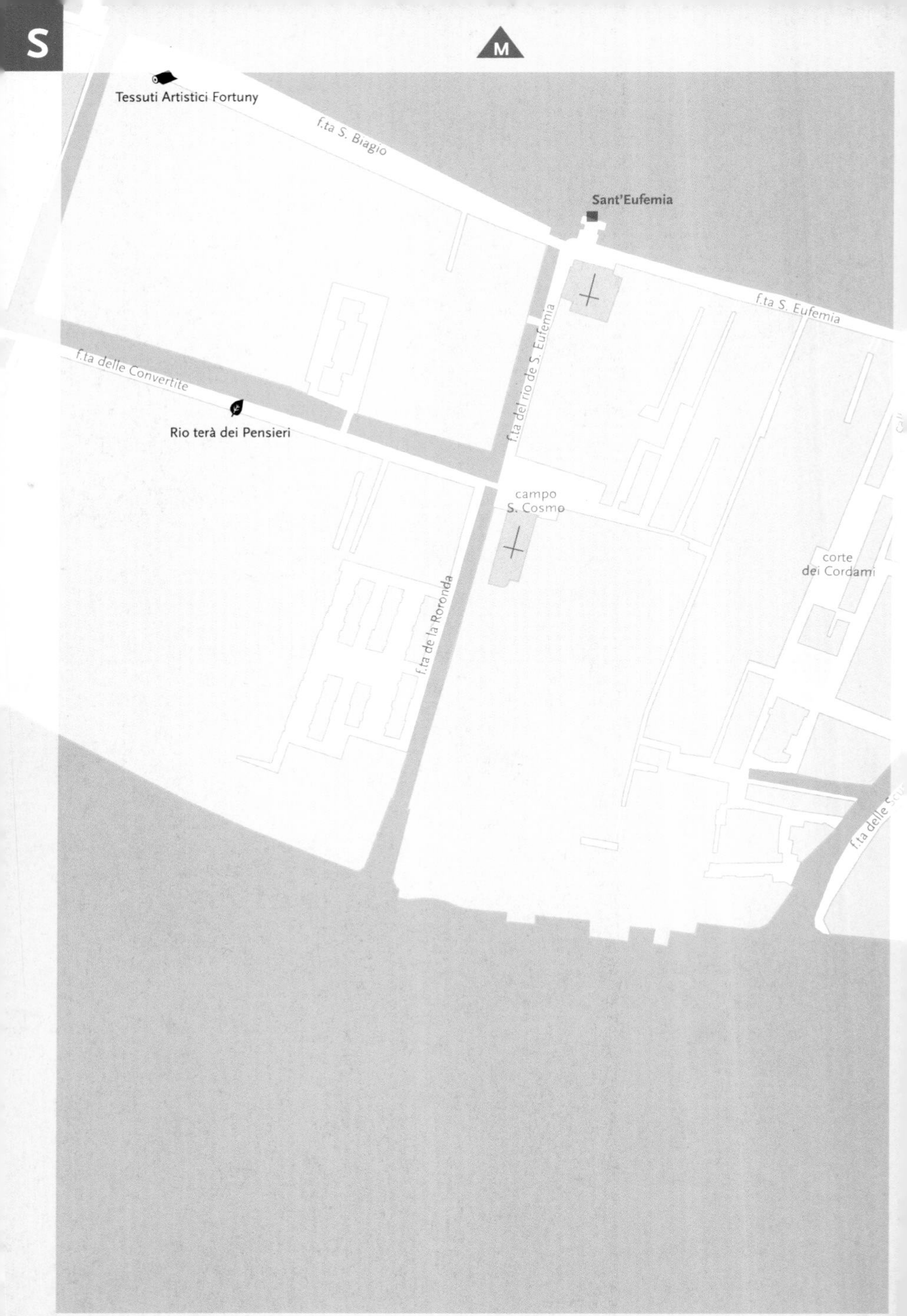

Tessuti Artistici Fortuny

f.ta S. Biagio

Sant'Eufemia

f.ta S. Eufemia

f.ta del rio de S. Eufemia

f.ta delle Convertite

Rio terà dei Pensieri

campo
S. Cosmo

f.ta de la Rotonda

corte
dei Cordami

f.ta delle Cro...

T

Canale della Giudecca

Giudecca

calle del Forno

calle de l'olio

f.ta del Ponte Piccolo

Ponte Longo

f.ta S. Giacomo

coop

calle larga Ferrando

calle de le Erbe

Spazio legno

campiello
Ferrando

f.ta de la Palada

calle S. Giacomo

le scuole

Crea

Dei Rossi

O

Alphabetical index